A SMALL BOY IN THE SIXTIES

A SMALL BOY IN THE SIXTIES

BY

GEORGE STURT

Author of
The Bettesworth Book, Change in the Village,
The Wheelwright's Shop, etc.

WITH
AN INTRODUCTION
BY
ARNOLD BENNETT

THE HARVESTER PRESS

This edition first published in 1977 by
THE HARVESTER PRESS LIMITED
Publisher: John Spiers
2 Stanford Terrace,
Hassocks, Sussex

British Library Cataloguing in Publication Data

Sturt, George
    A small boy in the sixties.
    1. Farnham, Surrey – Social life and customs
    I. Title
    942.2′19   DA690.F24

    ISBN 0 85527 244 9

Printed by Unwin Brothers Limited, Old Woking, Surrey.

CONTENTS

v

CONTENTS

INTRODUCTION

You can see from the frontispiece, which is a very good portrait, what George Sturt looked like. A dark man with regular features, fine benevolent eyes, and an old-fashioned dark beard. He was perhaps ever so slightly under the average height. His voice was low and effective; his demeanour modest, not shy, and not retiring—at any rate he only retired before what bored him or what he disdained. He was a bachelor, and lived during most of his life with his two maiden sisters in a small house with a small garden in a small village called The Lower Bourne, near Farnham, which is a good Surrey country town.

He travelled little, and never extensively. In a long series of his letters—1895 to 1922—which I possess, there is only one that is not dated from his house; the unique exception came from Edinburgh, whither I believe he had gone by sea. Even his visits to London were infrequent.

By trade he was a wheelwright (see his book *The Wheelwright's Shop*). He had a business in Farnham which he directed with the help of a partner. He once took me to his yard; it was quite a small yard, very similar to other yards; but George could make a wheel interesting. Wheels and the receptacles swung between them were to him exciting objects, and he could communicate the excitement which they aroused in himself. For the more tedious aspects of his business, such as making out bills and engaging office boys, George had but a moderate enthusiasm. He counted the day happy when he could avoid going into Farnham.

By profession he was an author. All his letters to me—and they are numerous—are mainly about the craft of putting things into words, for print. He had a pretty wide range, too. It is a common mistake to assume that because his best known work is concerned with the observation of rural manners, therefore his literary interests were limited to the same. He wrote at least two novels, *A Year's Exile* and *The Extinction of the Keens* (the latter was never published), and began one or two others. He was attracted by the drama, and began more than one farce. Also he dealt much in theories of aesthetic with a sociological trend (see for instance his book *The Ascending Effort*, in the value of which he deeply believed). He did reviews for *The Academy* under Lewis Hind.

As a rule he wrote slowly and with difficulty, and he got his work published slowly and with difficulty. But he did finish books, and he did get them published, and in the result the lettered public came to join in the very high appreciation in which he had for many years been held by the friends who intimately knew him and who could recognise authentic literature when they saw it.

But neither the public nor his friends have yet seen his chief work, which was his Journal. The origin of this work is obscure. On June 25th, 1896, George wrote to me: "I once kept a journal—a sickly, analytic thing containing some good stuff amidst much rubbish. And today...I hauled the old book out and wrote in it for those two hours I spoke of: a criticism of Stevenson."

So that there must have been a considerable hiatus in the keeping of the Journal. In those days, when I was myself beginning to keep a journal, I used to make and stitch and bind the virgin volumes with my own hands. George happened to see a volume, and he said that if he had a book like that to write in he would keep a journal regularly. I said: "I will make you a volume." I made him two volumes.

The Journal (new series) had not been commenced in December 1896, but in December 1906 it had reached its seventh volume. On February 22nd, 1908, it was still in the seventh volume. Under that date he wrote me of it: "It goes by fits and starts, and is not often narrative, but impressionist or analytic. It will be the most vividly interesting work I shall ever write; but it will not be published, probably, until I'm dead—excepting in bits which will be incorporated into schemed-out books."

In that last clause is the point—namely, that probably the Journal was, directly or indirectly, the basis of nearly all that George wrote after the commencement of the second series. I have never seen the Journal, but I am sure that it is very comprehensive in scope. He wrote to me on December 23rd, 1898: "Damme, I'm beastly interested in all sorts of things." Some of his letters give light on the way in which he kept the Journal. Thus, dated June 26th, 1898:

But, by Jingo! if one could get down to understand village life! I have reached that initiatory stage in which one is convinced of ignorance....It were almost as easy to write of the Chinese. Yet if one only could! I was counting up last night the elemental tragedy stuff that has occurred in the cottages within 100 yards from here, since I came here seven years ago. Here's the bald catalogue:

> 4 deaths of old men
> 2   „   young men, leaving families
> 1 death of a mother
> 1   „   an infant
> 1 case of sunstroke, with delirium
> 1   „   haemorrhage: fits (man still lying
>   between life and death)
> 1 girl home "in trouble."

The ingenious—almost devilish—torture of poverty is going [on] more or less all the time. All these affairs were more or less dramatic...."

And in the same letter:

It was not until yesterday evening—7.30—that I had any chance at writing, and in the interim yet another matter had come, for my journal—a bad accident in the village, with a side-light on village life. I wrote until dark. Then got my supper...and after it, intending to continue writing—looked out first at the night. Low voices in the lane could be heard. I stole down close to the hedge....A man and a girl—tentatively philandering, I suppose....That had to be entered in my journal forthwith—and it took me until 12.30 to get it down. Not until this morning were the notes on the Fair finished: and now the total addition to the journal, for the last 24 hours, is about 21 pages—say about 3000 words. Not much "literature" in it. But documentary stuff.

George Sturt was always thus fervently in pursuit of knowledge about the English labouring class. The man whom he called Bettesworth in *The Bettesworth Book*, who worked in his garden and whom I was once asked to

x

meet, was a hero for him—and I consider justifiably. And perhaps his chief heroine in life was Mrs Bettesworth. He never condescended to these people, either in intercourse or in thought. Nor did he regard them as "quaint." Nothing was more likely to anger him than a condescending attitude towards them, with a gently "tickled" appreciation of their alleged quaintness. In September 1900 a clergyman aroused his resentment by some written remarks and suggestions about the material in *The Bettesworth Book*, and George wrote me, after admitting the fairness of certain criticisms:

But when he talks about "the old fellow's quaint narratives" then I behold the country parson in whose sight a man like Bettesworth has next to no virtues and is either coarse or "quaint." If my book has enough of the real man in it to grate on a parson's nerves, then perhaps it should not be altered. When one thinks of it, the mere notion of submitting such a man as Bettesworth (even in a report of him) to the judgment of a parson is absurd.... You twig his idea of reconstruction: it's to be *my* notes and appreciation of the "country life." He wants *me* to come and entertain him in his study with anecdotes of the quaint old fellows in the village, so that we may smile over 'em together, and then sigh, and be struck perhaps by "a thought" for tomorrow's sermon.... The pity is that the parson and his set have to be considered, so that a man can't try to publish sundry things about labouring people which are by no means "quaint."

The real, inmost George Sturt shows in those lines. He had a steely and everlasting hatred of all sentimentality. He said what he thought, or he said nothing. To his friends he said everything, even about his friends. His external mildness, his unshakable politeness, were misleading. You might not altogether like knowing where you were with him, but you did know where you were with him. "This is unworthy of you," he would write, of a piece of your work. Consequently he inspired passionate loyalties in his friends.

In 1916 he broke a blood-vessel at the base of his brain and was almost helpless for a time. But in a few months he was on the way to recovery, and had resumed correspondence. The handwriting, however, showed a mortal change from the wonderfully neat and legible script of former days. In January 1917 he had even formed a hope of coming to London. Then the handwriting improved again. But on March 23rd, 1920, he wrote: "And further, about a fortnight ago, blowed or blest (you know what I mean!) if I didn't have another slight stroke, which has left me all but helpless." On May 7th, 1922, he wrote: "I can scarcely move across the room now...and an hour's chatter reduces me to mumbling. But I giggle a good deal; keep cheerful; and am enjoying life intensely. ...I see quite a number of people too—local people... those undistinguished nobodies who are displaying to me (though they don't suspect it) what normal English have got in 'em."

This was the last time I heard from him direct. He died on February 4th, 1927.

ARNOLD BENNETT

AUTHOR'S PREFACE

THIS book was hardly finished when around the memories it deals with grew an idea which may as well be set down here in the following prefatory notes as it has no proper place elsewhere, yet may help the whole. Briefly, the memories are of two sorts, besides the reflections commenting on them, which in fact are not memories at all. The reflections are left, in the hope that they may kindle light on the little things remembered. For instance, the cantankerous geniality—kindly, though pig-headed—of the mid-Victorian town-life, considered now, restores many of the details remembered and is itself lit up by them, until an air almost of the eighteenth century seems to have lingered in the Farnham of the eighteen-sixties. Again, I think that the meadows and hop-grounds, the ancient streets, and the countrified traffic and affairs, are better to be appreciated, if the quiet that used to rest over them is noticed now. Yet the eighteenth century doggedness and the still more ancient quiet ought not to be classed exactly as memories. I give them now, at any rate, rather as reflections of after years, illustrating and illustrated by things recalled.

Of actual memories there are, as already said, two distinct kinds to be noted. The first kind is made up of the minutest sensations or perceptions, repeated so often that the sort of child I was could hardly miss noticing them in time, until at last their appeal grew familiar, and can be more exactly considered to-day. Thus there was the limpid caress everywhere of the daylight. I realise now how excellent it was, and how it pervaded my childhood, though I hardly noticed it then, but took it for granted. Likewise I took for granted the procession of expected changes, from Sunday round to Sunday again, or from May-day to Squib-night; or the coming of the Fairs, and so on, through those vanished years. These items yield a similar delight to the daylight and recur now to my mind in much the same way. Or, once more, in the category of pleasing sensations experienced over and over again until I began to "know what I liked," are certain attributes now singled-out and identified—the colours of meadow or woodland or heath, of cloud or distance; the shapes of fossils or fruit, or of animals or of limbs, of Greek casts, of gentle valleys. The quality of sounds, wind, rain, horses trotting; the lines traced by things in motion—balls, birds' flights, "ducks and drakes" and so on. All these things left their momentary impression, to be more consciously noted at last and to be enjoyed now.

But, while these enjoyments were too frequent to be long ignored and books and pictures drew additional attention to them, there were other experiences in quite a separate class—incidents not repeated at all. And a very noteworthy circumstance is connected with my memories of these unexpected incidents. The notable point is this. Occasions when I was alone, though they cannot have been infrequent, are not plentifully recalled. I infer therefore that in solitude my attention was but sluggish. On the other hand, I do recall many occasions when other people were with me and were presumably directing their senses the same way as mine. Was I, then, using their perceptions rather than my own? Reading our environment through their eyes? Interpreting what was happening by other people's behaviour? Were signs of amusement enough to amuse me? or of fear to alarm me? Individual animals gathered together depend on one another's understanding—sheep on the Downs, birds on the ploughed land, tiny fish in the brook. Grown-up people do it too— in the street, when they stop to see what somebody else is staring at; in a 'bus, when a fellow-passenger's laugh with the conductor sets them happily smiling, although they have themselves missed the joke. Your very dog or cat may get reassurance from your eyes or your behaviour, though the circumstances that caused timidity are not changed. And it seems likely that a child, too, being a little animal, has a wary eye on his fellows and is swayed by their apparent understanding—an understanding which he may or may not verify for himself afterwards, even as the sheep, the starlings, the sudden minnows; or as the people in the street, the passengers in the 'bus, the dog or cat. Such understanding in fact seems to be a part of human nature that is not too often guessed yet is as important to the individual as the swarm is to any ant or bee. This at least, I fancy, indicates how a number of the sensations now recalled grew intense enough to survive at all in my memory. They are a child's readings, through other people's eyes, of what was going on around him in old days.

Whether, as is not impossible, memories of this kind, largely independent of individuals, make up the half impersonal life of local and national tradition, of folk-lore, of craftsmanship, is hardly to be considered here; still less is this the place for opening up the questions that occur, as to a new valuation of the importance of individuals if they could be shown-up against the undying life of the little communities they belong to; or the importance of holidays, travel, and cognate questions. None of that need intrude here. Here rather is at best only a picture of such a little bit of undying life, obscure though hardly dull, as it looked to a child in Victorian days. It is at least truthful.

G. S.

CHAPTER I

AT 18 BOROUGH

"18 Borough" (now rebuilt in Mr H. K. Bentall's shop) had six rooms, besides a wash-house at the back. The downstairs room on the street had a shop-window its full width—ten feet or so—at one side of the street door; and on the other side of this door was "The Shutter Hole." This, a narrow cupboard opening on to the street—a cupboard some two feet wide perhaps and three or four feet deep (I think I never went into it)—this Shutter Hole had once been a watchman's shelter, they said; but so far as I know it was never used for anything but to store the shop shutters—those artfully grained shutters—when they were taken down every morning and put away for the day.

The shop-window was probably partitioned off from the shop by sliding glass casements. I cannot remember this; but a memory of dull red woodwork—cheap Venetian red—runs into the lines of casement frames such as would suit there. Outside, the shop-window glass did not reach lower than some two feet or so above the street pavement. At this height the window ledge began, on the outside. My sister had, when a tiny girl, laid pennies from the shop till along the whole length of the ledge—very nice they must have looked to any passer-by in the street. Within, I fancy, the bottom of the casement gave the level for a boarded floor to the window; and in the two feet of darkness under these boards were not bundles of old unsold newspapers stored?

A counter ran the greater part of the length of the shop. It covered sundry drawers. One of these drawers was the shop till; in another were halfpenny pen-holders, steel pen boxes ("magnum bonums" had yellow pen-sticks); and there were penny cedar ("seedy") pencils, slate pencils (some of them covered with paper), wafers, sticks of sealing wax, india-rubber, ink-eraser, elastic bands, quill pens—all sorts of interesting things. Other items of stock that should not be forgotten were box-lining paper, printed with little spots or stars of blue, fire-screens—long tresses of curly coloured paper—and choice kinds of note-paper with "gophered edges" if you wished to be very chic, or if you were to write a love letter. For mourning, black-edged paper and envelopes might even show the extent of the bereavement—the black edge being so wide as to leave but scanty room for a few words of grief, if a very near relative had died. One very curious request would some-times come from a villager; the man or woman asking for "a head." What was meant was a penny postage stamp, bearing a profile of Queen Victoria's head. In the shop, too, was kept for the convenience of customers a supply of the twopenny pale mauve Receipt Stamps more than twice the size of a postage stamp—which would do for a receipt in those days. There was also perforated cardboard, in which you might, with a sharp knife point, cut out highly refined patterns that would show well on blue silk, and so make a dainty book-marker or needle-case for a Christmas present.

On the floor under the counter stood the gas meter, in a cavernous darkness. The place served me well for a cave; and as I spent a lot of time on the floor and in that cave, of course I knew that the gas meter had in front of it two jolly little clock faces as I thought, with hands that could be pushed round to please one's taste. Why there was no glass over these dials I do not know; nor yet do I know that my occasional adjustment of the hands was ever found out. The floor behind the counter had a knot-hole in it. Once I caught a blue-bottle fly and put it down into that knot-hole. Only once. My hands smelt so disagreeably of the fly that the sport was not worth repeating.

At the inner end of the shop was a number of books. The books had probably been chosen by my father, with nothing to guide him save his own unusual and far from ordinary or popular taste. Probably there were not a dozen other men in the town who cared for reading at all. I recall an argument between one of these and my father as to whether the *n* in "contemporary" should be pronounced; or elided, as my father held. But this must have been at a somewhat later stage than these other earliest recollections; probably of the period when I liked to look at *The Young Men of Great Britain*, for the sake of its pictures of Red Indians—a journal for some reason frowned upon by the seniors, but to my taste, far more attractive than *The Boys of England* substituted for it. These two journals could sometimes be found by rummaging in the piles stacked away in the dark under the shop window.

Perhaps the date of these interests of mine was round about 1870–71. I used then (lying on the floor in the inner room) to wonder why *The Illustrated London News* always referred to the Franco-Prussian War as the "Military" War. What other sort of war was there? The pictures struck me as dull and all alike. There was one, however, a large picture—of some "petroleuses" being shot. It seemed a shame. Then, I think, is when I first heard the name of Louise Michel. I had a sort of partisan contempt for the new French gun, the Mitrailleuse, a sort of partisan approval of the Prussian Needle-gun. It must have been during the Siege of Paris that I heard a lady in the shop (Miss Knight, then or soon afterwards Mrs Shalden Smith), exclaim to a friend, "Oh! *Poor* Pari(s)." Several names became familiar to me—Bismarck, the Crown Prince, Bazaine.

During the same period Farnham Streets still echoed sometimes with reminders of the American Civil War—whenever wretched Street-singers wandered along wailing "Just Before the Battle Mother." In the same way I learnt the tune (but I have forgotten it now) of

Oh the King of Abyssinia,
Oh the very wicked King!

(Can I have been taken to London at this stage? I have a recollection of seeing a "Transformation Scene," in which a huge face—"King Theodore's"—emerged out of chaos on a curtain at a theatre. It was at the Regent Street Polytechnic, where also was a wonderful diving bell, and a man blowing glass in a side room all by himself. Then too, at intervals all round the walls of the main building, were fascinating peepholes into tiny galleries where little toy coal-trucks went running by on toy rails.)

4

It must have been at about this same stage of my growth that my attention was seized by a very crude drawing in red chalk, on the stuccoed wall of "The Surrey Arms" in East Street. Why did it fix itself in my memory? I seem to see it now—colour, position and all. The face was but a profile about as big as half-a-crown. Near it was written the word "Fenian," which I was able to read. And as this is absolutely all that I can remember about the circumstance, I can only surmise that there must have been some strong public feeling connected with it, to stamp so trivial a matter so indelibly on my memory.

One other public matter of about this period has not been quite forgotten—a parliamentary election. A disquiet of excitement in the staid old street clings to my dim thought of it—a boy I probably knew was singing an election song:

> I wish I had a penny.
> What for? What for?
> To buy a rope to hang the pope,
> And Pennington for ever.

The tune recurs with the words. But what it was all about I don't know. Was Pennington to be hanged for ever? He was one of the candidates. There were two others— Cubitt, and Briscow.

A Mr George Peacock, probably coming for his morning newspaper in those far-away days, used to call me "Copper-toes," because the toes of my little boots were covered with narrow strips of copper to keep them from wearing out too fast. A curious man was Mr Peacock. My father and mother dubbed his manner "theatrical," perhaps because of his strutting walk, and his swinging his cane up to his shoulder, in gay swishing movement. He lived at the house in front of what is now Barling's "Castle Brewery," of which he was, I fancy, the owner at that time.

It may have been a little later, but I was certainly very young when I had a bitter disappointment over some knickerbockers. I do not remember caring much about such matters at any other time, before or since. True, in after years the acquisition of my first trousers satisfied me —they would allow me to walk through stinging-nettles without getting my legs stung. But that, though so desirable a thing, was only a utility; whereas, at the time referred to, I seem to have been affected for once by an interest in the appearance of my clothes. The occasion was the conversion to my use of a pair of my brother's discarded knickerbockers. Now had they been passed over to me as they were, they would have hung down, I judged, to my ankles just like trousers. But my benighted Aunt Ann could not be persuaded to leave well alone. She insisted on cutting off the legs so as to reduce the garment again to knickerbockers for me. I was bitterly disappointed.

Behind the shop, and separated from it only by a narrow staircase, was the "sitting-room"; and behind that again (outside a latched ledge door) was the wash-house and yard. In fact, this sitting-room (like the little shop also) was no more than a widening of the passage to the back premises from the street.

A frequent nuisance, to me, was the weekly washing. It should be understood that my mother, though there was a small servant-girl, had more than enough to do at minding the shop, house-maiding, cooking, mending and making clothes for the family, and generally keeping the house going. She carried on a biggish correspondence with her own mother and sisters; she helped (and was helped by) my father in all the household accounts and economies; she kept her eye on us children and our upbringing.

So it was natural enough that for the family washing a washer-woman was hired—a Mrs Weymouth's name recurs to me. To be sure, my mother helped with the wringing and drying, to say nothing of the subsequent ironing; but she got Mrs Weymouth or another to do the work at the wash-tub. And to myself the unpleasing thing was as follows:

At dinner-time the washer-woman was called in to sit down to dinner with the rest of us. Now, I had no class prejudices then (my father and mother would have laughed it out of me, if I had thought of such a thing), but I did object to Mrs Weymouth's damp apron (blue print) and to her fingers all flabby and wrinkled from the soapsuds. My brother, I believe, fairly yelled once at sitting to dinner with such a being. I was not so bad as that. But my disgust must have been very keen. As if by some association with discomfort, for years afterwards a certain sort of unpalatable food (underdone cold mutton) always seemed to me to taste "like washer-women's aprons," I was wont to say.

One day news came that Mrs Weymouth was dead. She had broken a blood-vessel in her leg, they said. It was the first time I had ever heard of such a thing.

7

But, beyond the discomforts already told of, I do not remember any others in this poky little home. On the contrary it was almost all happiness for me there. I feel as if I was one of those blissfully-placed children Oscar Pletsch used to draw, in his domestic scenes. Things went cheerfully; everything was interesting—my sister's dolls, the clothes drying over the fire-guard, my mother's starching and ironing; or the preparations for dinner.

As I recall it, it seems as if summer always lay over that little shaded back room behind the shuttered shop— summer quiet in the outlook along the shadowed back-yard towards the distant tree-tops of Farnham Park. Yet, through this memory as of perpetual June, I seem to see my father, in his Sunday clothes back from church, stripping off his black gloves and bending down to warm his hands by the winter fire. For some of his fingers were "dead," he said: and indeed they looked bloodless, corpse-like.

More interesting however than the real cookery was my own play cookery. In front of the sitting-room fire, across a narrow hearth-rug, stood the dinner table. My mother could hear thence if anyone came into the shop; and while she worked there amongst the pots and pans (I still seem to see the pan of flour, the highly-glazed red earthenware) I at her side was busy too. I was at work on a little scrap of pastry making it thin, cutting-out little disks of it with my mother's thimble (in which a disk often stuck, until it was howked out perhaps on to the floor), and then stamping a pattern on each disk with the thimble-top. After the pastry had been cut out into a limp network it could be rolled together between my hands, and then flattened out to make three or four more cuttings. Finally the disks, arranged on a plate, were put into the oven to be baked. If then I did not wholly forget them they would eventually be taken out—cold, dry, flinty, and usually grey from their frequent visits to the hearth-rug. Yet I ate them.

What would one not eat in those days? With my brother I went into a little grimy tent at Farnham fair. A conjuror there, borrowing a hat (probably some villager's old beaver) mixed and cooked in it a currant pudding to everybody's great astonishment. But, my brother says, he for his part ate some of that pudding!

I do not remember that treat, myself. But I did often enjoy cabbage-stumps, which my mother cut from the cabbages she was preparing for dinner, and put (for me) in a glass of water on the window-sill of the wash-house. I also had a liking for a slither of uncooked ham "in my fingers," and for a certain curranty pudding before it was cooked. Sometimes, on a Sunday, half a table-spoonful of gravy from roast mutton or beef was given me, before the joint was taken away, but the "liquor" from salt pork was poured over one's slice of plum pudding and made it very palatable.

I liked to watch my mother making fritters for Shrove Tuesday. She put a little beer into them! An experiment of salt fish—perhaps for one Ash Wednesday—was not repeated. As we had breakfasted by half past seven, when the morning papers came, and dinner was not till after my father could get back from his wheelwright's shop at one

9

o'clock, we perhaps stood more in need than most people of the eleven o'clock "lunch" which everybody we knew took as a regular thing. Hot elderberry-wine, in the winter, was an accompaniment to our bread and cheese then. The wine was in tallish glasses—about twice the height of an ordinary wine-glass; and a finger of toast sopped in it was pleasant eating. At dinner I almost welcomed cold meat if there chanced to be mashed potatoes. For an "oven" could be chopped into the mash, where a mouthful of meat, buried for a few minutes, might with luck become almost tepid again. And if that was not in itself super-latively nice, it was all the same very nice indeed to be playing at "ovens" with one's food. Similarly nice—not for itself, but because it was odd—was an Osborne biscuit sopped in one's tea.

One queer thing comes back to my thoughts. In the shop, besides the double gas pendant over the counter, a gas bracket stood out over a little desk near the inner door. To this bracket, which, having no globe (there were none in the shop) offered the most accessible flame, I would run out from my supper o' winter nights, to toast a mouthful of cheese. I probably burnt it, holding it on a fork right in the flame; but even so it was nicer than any toasted cheese I have tasted since.

From my mother's farm-house home came now and then a home-made loaf; a "Lardy" cake—all flaky; a quarter of a large currant cake too full of lemon-peel for my taste; a supply of "scraps" for mince-meat; a hog's pudding or two; souse; a corking of hocks, and once (ah how succulent!) a dish of chitterlings ("chidlins"). A goodly number of apples—"Lady's Fingers" came once or twice from the same source. They looked green, but were in fact very good eating. Little Siberian crabs that sometimes came instead were nothing like so nice, though better to see.

Thin biscuits—a sort of shortbread—made for us by my grandmother herself and known as "Grandmother's biscuits" were a treat. I am also glad in this connection to recall how good were the dough buns that often came from my uncle's at Frensham, tastier far (besides more frequent) than the hot-cross buns bought from the bakery, of course, on Good Friday only.

Sometimes I was sent to a grocer's to get samples of cheese, and these were brought home to try—small cylinders about as big as your little finger—wrapped round in a bit of paper and marked with the price. Dutch cheese (with attractive red rind), Cheddar, American—I was acquainted with various kinds, and liked to watch the grocer scooping out the samples with his knowing "Cheesetaster"—a sort of gimlet without a nose, kept for that use. (Sundry other tradesmen's tools were familiar to me— sugar-nippers for cutting loaf sugar into manageable lumps, the flencher we had in our cellar for getting out a glass full of the home-made wine, for sampling; but cheese-tasters, if only I could have had one of my own, were the best of all.) Sometimes the cheese produced a curious dust which my father used to show us (under his cheap microscope) to be furnished with legs; and sometimes it even yielded little pale maggots. But, by the way, the very bacon could grow maggoty, with jumping "bacon

11

hoppers." Yet maggoty bacon was not so nasty as rusty bacon.

Of sweets ("lollipops") I had not many. Acid-drops (sometimes replaced by pear-drops or raspberry-drops) were the best known. There were also sugar-sticks, hard-bake, butter-scotch in long plaited twists, and sugar-candy. This last named (broken into small mouthfuls or even into dust with a hammer) gave interest to the otherwise rather tiresome home industries of making wine, especially grape-wine. (Now and again a grape popped into my mouth made me wish my mother would not spoil all those nice bunches—white grapes they were—in the tub, by crushing them under her flat-iron.)

At the back of the dwelling-house, shading the little narrow yard, ran a short string of outbuildings—wash-house, "copper-hole," "shed."

From the street the way to these back premises was through the shop, and then through the sitting-room or living-room—shop and living-room being, as already said, merely widenings (on the right) of the straight passage through from street to back. Anyone passing along the street and glancing through the shop-door might have seen, at the further end of the sitting-room, the back-door; or, if that were open, right along to the fire-grate at the end of the wash-house; for the wash-house was only divided from the sitting-room by the back-door.

Before thinking my way back into the yard, where I spent so many delightful hours, I would like to look round a little further at that tiny scullery. It was here, at the fire-grate at the far end, that my mother, on Shrove Tuesday made the fritters—pancakes, I called them,—mentioned before. There must have been a table somewhere, but I don't know where it stood, unless under the window between fire-place and back-door. This window—longish though shallow—had light from the yard outside; but the window-panes were of green bottle-glass, and nobody could look in or out. On the window-sill those cabbage-stumps I have already referred to were put; there too I grew used to seeing, at one period, a bottle of Dr de Jongh's Light-brown Cod-liver Oil, fishy-flavoured stuff, supposed to be tasteless. The scullery had no ceiling, but the rafters (with slates showing between them) were at least out of headway.

You had to go out into the yard, passing (outside) by the bottle-glass wash-house window, to get to the next place—the "copper-hole." This place deserved its name; a "hole" it was—a low and narrow room with one side left out. In fact it was but a shallow pit, below the level of the yard, overflow water from the yard being kept out by a sill of paving bricks. From the yard a step over this sill brought one down upon the brick floor of the copper-hole. Here, with its flue of course joining the wash-house chimney, was the copper itself, in use every washing day, while the washing tubs (not galvanized iron but heavy oak tubs) and the stool for them stood close by. Nor was washing the only use for the copper and copper-hole. Here, periodically, my father did his brewing, as was the way with most householders of the time; and certain brewing utensils—a mash-tub, a funnel and sundry other things (all of wood)—stood along with the wash-tubs. How sweet the place smelt sometimes! And what fun it was to see the new beer (when at last the plug was knocked out of the mash-tub) spirt out into the shallow cooling-tub on the floor! My father had some sovereign dodge for knowing the right heat for a part of the process: when he could see his face reflected in the mash-tub (or perhaps it was in the copper), that was a sign that the steam had gone off enough for this or that to be done. I may have known at the time what this next thing was, but I have quite forgotten now. All that is left to me of these delectable times (the more delectable because my father was at home) is an impression of busy and peaceful work, in fragrant air and soft autumn daylight. The season was almost certainly autumn, while the daylight was sunshine reflected back across our yard from our neighbour's out-houses into the brickwork copper-hole. As that place faced eastwards only the earliest morning sun-rays can have shone straight into it. But later in the day a quieter light came in limpid and refreshing. The clouds of white steam which I remember billowing across the yard probably rose from the washing. Of my mother's wine-making the only reason I have for associating the copper-hole with it is a sort of mental picture of grapes in a shallow tub, standing on a floor of paving-bricks. After the copper-hole (a step further along the yard) was the "shed"—as dusty and rubbishy as the other place was neat.

The knife-cleaning and the boot-blacking carried on here will be told of by and by. The "shed" was probably a "glory-hole" for old packing-paper, ends of string, and any other litter from the shop; but I have no clear recollection of any of this. Half-way along it (and that can have been but a stride) lay "chips" from my father's wheel-wright's shop—chips from spoke-dressing, little blocks of oak or ash or elm or beech, curly shavings of dry timber—all most excellent for fire lighting. And beyond the chips, in the farthest and darkest corner of the shed (the "coal-hole") was half a ton or so of coal. Coal, chips, boots, litter, knife-cleaning, dust—they all contributed to a fine confusion.

Slanting up atop of the heap of coal, a short step-ladder reached to a hole in an upper floor but reached no further. At the top it was necessary to clamber across as best one could, before one could stand up in "the loft," an ample sky-light in the eastern slope of the roof let the light in pleasantly: and this skylight gave my father opportunity to indulge a taste otherwise starved. For, under the glass, on a staging he had hung there, he was able to rear a few greenhouse plants. Balsams, very green and juicy, with pretty gay flowers, make a sort of picture in my memory still. Just after breakfast he used to water them—thinking of it I get a sensation of nice wet coolness—and he probably raised other plants: my memory is of balsams and calceo-larias and geraniums and dripping water. Somewhere near by was an old packing case full of potting-earth, often dry.

This loft was prolonged, down a step or two, to an inner loft over the copper-hole. No skylight was here, but a window low enough even for me; and, I suspect, not glazed. At least there was no glass there when, with my brother and a certain school-fellow of his (now an esteemed Farnham citizen) I used a peashooter, aiming excitedly at nothing, up and down the yard just below me. On some shallow shelves at the end of this inner loft was a stack of little green-covered pamphlets. But how disappointing! They were many copies of the same number of some dreary missionary report! Again and again I hunted through them for a change; yet always in vain. Somebody had blundered in the shop—and this was the sorry result. A wretched little wood-cut of a black man is all that memory now preserves from my frequent searches.

But now for the yard itself. "Our yard is hatchet shate," was the first sentence in my first essay; and I don't know how better to describe the yard now, excepting that the last word would be better spelt "shape." I never understood why my father laughed at this eight year old effort of mine; I feel sure it only recorded what he himself had more than once said. He, the skilled mechanic, who could do much with an axe that men try to do with a saw now-a-days, said "our yard" was shaped like a hatchet, and so it was. From the sitting-room window you looked down the length of the yard—the handle of the hatchet—from end to end; but at the far end, past the shed, the narrow and shady "handle" led to a squarish and sunnier space—"the head" of the supposed hatchet. In this space, round the corner and decently out of sight from the dwelling house, was the privy, not more than twenty yards or so away from the house, but far enough, of course, on a rainy night or if the yard was covered with snow. This little place did but occupy one corner of the "head" of the hatchet-shaped yard. Beside it was a rockery, where grew English marigolds, with a scent I never smell now without getting back to childhood. And near the rockery was a foot or so of ground where once, imitating my father, I stuck in a piece of geranium stem and, behold, it "struck"! Oh, but I was proud!

The yard, like the side-walks to the streets throughout Farnham town then, was paved with iron-stones set-in on edge. Up and down this narrow space (there can hardly have been six feet of width to it) my sister delighted to troll her wooden hoop; but the stones would have made my iron hoop too noisy, even for me. Still, there was room for fun: I managed to play at what we called "cricket" there. Palings—close slate-coloured palings some five or six feet high—separated "our yard" from Bolland's similar yard next door; and too often the ball "went over." Of course balls will do that. It's a tiresome way they have, as I learnt later at school. Still, the yard sufficed for "cricket." But a shuttlecock could hardly be used—the least little wind sent it "over" too persistently.

Two or three times my father brought home from his wheelwright's shop a round disk of thick leather—no doubt the waste middle of some large cart-washer—a disk two inches across, perhaps. After this had been threaded on to a stout piece of string and thoroughly soaked in water until it was lissom, it made no end of a fine sucker, and with admiration I watched while my father pressed all the edges of the leather to any piece of wood—the fence, the door—and gave me leave to try to pull it away by pulling at the central string. He himself fixed the sucker on to the bottom of an upturned wooden pail, and so carried the pail away. Another time, laying a shilling—or perhaps a halfpenny—on the dry bottom of a tub (or I think it must have been a red earthenware pan, to leave in my memory such a glistening picture of wet glaze) and causing me to stand just far enough back to lose sight of the coin, he brought it surprisingly into my vision again, simply by pouring clear water over it. It may have been due to such help that I was ready, by and by, to take the meaning of Tennyson's "Straight staff bent in a pool." I had often, in our back-yard, seen a stick—perhaps it was the copper-stick—bend upwards in a different angle, at the surface of any water it was plunged into.

One other wonderful thing my father did in that yard, not to amuse me but to lighten his own labour. It has been told how he brewed beer. This beer eventually had to be got down into a barrel, in a cellar under the sitting-room, to which cellar stairs led down—dark and inconvenient stairs—if one wanted to go there. But my father did not want to go there himself: he only wanted to get the beer down into the barrel. To carry it down the stairs would have involved crossing the sitting-room from the back-door many times—tramping to and fro over the hearth rug to the cellar door at the inner corner of the sitting-room. But my father avoided all this. With a piece of gas piping, that would bend in his hands, he made a siphon. From the new beer in the copper-hole the siphon passed, through a grating in the yard over the cellar window, down to the barrel below. And if it was a sort of miracle—as it was—to see the beer putting itself away, my father cared to let us children understand how he worked it.

Inside the sitting-room window, blocking the view from there all down the length of the yard, he built for himself, in slight mahogany framework and slender angle-iron and carriage-window glass, a fern-case which was his delight. Even as in the loft he tended his balsams, so here in the sitting-room he lovingly ministered to his maidenhairs and spleenworts, lifting them out to be watered and, if need be, trimmed with scissors. No trouble was too much for my father. From him I learnt a few common fern names: imitating him I hunted for ferns in odd country nooks which otherwise I should have passed by. If any delight in rural things has come into my life at all—and what a lot it has been, and how eager!—I owe more than a little of it to my father's fernery.

Dividing the shop from the sitting-room a steep and narrow flight of stairs led up to two rooms on the first floor —the "Front Room" over the shop and (at back) a bedroom. It was but a skip—I often skipped it—across the landing at the top of the stairs from one of these rooms to the other; but how agile one felt taking that skip! I remember feeling actually conscious that my agility was pleasant to me.

Of the bedroom I recall not so much as I might. I think I was not tall enough to see out of the window from it down into the back yard; besides, a child's interest in a bed is merely to sleep in. Yet I was tall enough to steady myself with my finger tips at the bedroom ceiling, when I chose to take an adventurous walk along the foot-rail at the bottom of the mahogany bedstead. There was a tester hung with damask curtains at the other end, over the pillows. Lying between those curtains, I often looked at some tall leaf-shapes contained in their pattern, and gave names to these shapes—Aunt Caroline, Aunt Eliza, Aunt

This, Aunt That. There were enough Aunts, and enough shapes (in solemn series) to match. And I lay awake in the bed, empty-headed, wide-eyed, looking, tallying.

My trouble was asthma, left behind by whooping-cough before I was twelve months old, as I have been assured. Often I have been lifted from my own little iron-framed bed in the corner into the damask-curtained bed, that my mother there might hold me up in her arms to ease the wheezing breath. Once she took me to a physician—a Dr Habershon—in London, for his advice. I was interested in the soft-piled red carpet of his consulting room. "Chronic bronchitis" was the name he gave to the disorder; and the treatment he advised included a deal of bread and milk. Unfortunately I did not much like that form of food, and would not try it as a part of my cure; and possibly the trouble was in fact digestive. Yet subsequently I have fancied excitement was at the bottom of it. I could not sleep away from home. Every Christmas, one night at least was spent at my mother's home at Farnborough; where I was so sure to have "a bad night" that Farnborough air was supposed not to suit me. It is more likely that I ate too much of the farmhouse fare.

Probably the asthma or indigestion had its roots, as already said, in the excitement of going on a visit at all and sleeping in a strange bed. Be this as it may, I often had to be held up in my mother's arms in the damask-curtained bed at Farnham. There, one night, I had a great fright.

Beside the bed stood a high chest of drawers, with two or three medicine phials on it—one of them containing ipecacuanha wine, supposed to be helpful in an attack of asthma. It ought to have been, truly! How well I remember, after half a century, the hateful twisting grip in my mouth of "ipecac," as we called it! The horrible taste was familiar; I was never in any doubt about it.

And so, on the night in question, I knew that it was something else I had sipped from the spoon, and not "ipecac" at all. My mother, overdone with her day's work, and now tired out yet waking to help me, had made a mistake and taken the wrong bottle. I can still hear her frightened cry to my father—"I have given the child hartshorn!" I do not know what had aroused her to her error. My father hurried to Doctor Clarke's, two streets away, and quickly brought back the advice to give me some form (I forget what) of yolk of egg. Meanwhile I had resigned myself, after some minutes of anxiety, to an expectation that I should soon be dead. It seemed to matter surprisingly little. Moreover, the shock had at least cured the asthma for the time being. And after all there was nothing in it. The two or three drops of hartshorn mistaken for ipecacuanha wine were in fact half perished in strength and caused me no discomfort. No doubt my mother suffered, and my father too, called up in the dark. But I remember only the interest of the candle-lit bedroom and being a centre of commotion. Finally a green but very sweet apple ("Lady's Finger") soothed my nerves and allowed the asthma to return; but more than this I do not remember.

The room just across the landing went by the name of the "Front Room." Any attempt to call it the "Drawing Room" was simply ignored: we had no use for pretence of grandeur. None the less, this was a sort of superior living-room, kept for important occasions and for Sundays.

The important occasions were the visits of aunts or uncles. "Lunch"—a sponge cake and a glass of home-made wine—was got for them in the Front Room; and while they sat in the sunshine (the day was always sunny when they came) it was a treat to sit by and sometimes get a taste of sponge cake.

In the Front Room was placed the new piano for my sister. My own delight in this acquisition went no further than to imagine what fine games of lions might be enjoyed, climbing along that shut up lid, when at last the piano should be worn out. It seemed to me I should always want to be a lion. Yet in time I did like to recognise tunes I knew, especially hymn-tunes on Sundays. "Art thou Weary" calls still to a queer sort of sentiment—a sacred-tune sort of sentiment—that took colour in me from that period. "Tell me the old old story" goes with it. "Calmly the Christian Martyr Sleeps" was the beginning of a song to which, indirectly, I owed a little enlightenment. For the "piece of music" recording the song had, outside, a picture of the Christian Martyr—a drowned young woman "sleeping calmly" on the water. But when I approved that mode of getting to Heaven—for I had not heard of a martyr before—my brother damped my ardour, by explaining that somebody else had to do the killing; one must by no means do it one's-self. On those terms martyrdom seemed no great catch after all.

On Sundays we had breakfast in the Front Room, a dough cake with currants or carraway seeds being an invariable part of the breakfast. One slice each—that was all. Bread and butter (or, when one was old enough to be allowed a knife, "bread and dab-it"—butter dabbed on with every mouthful—for we got butter direct from local farmers) made the rest of the meal. After breakfast, if one didn't go to church, one could sit by the window watching townsfolk going, or sit by the fire in winter-time, looking at picture-books or playing quietly with toys. Amongst the picture-books was, once, a Christmas Number of *The Bookseller*; and in it was a picture of a Hebrew prophet sitting on a donkey, and a lion near by. There seemed something sacred in this: something fit for Sunday and illustrative of the Bible. And anyhow the lion made an impression on me. I was certainly great on lions, in those days.

Or there were quiet toys. One, a little chip model of a farmstead, with a couple of very green trees, contained a diminutive barn or shed into which, as you peeped into the window, the daylight had stolen (you saw) with wonderful tranquillity. How I loved that reflected light! There, for the first time it seems to me—in that little two-inch toy— I tasted the amplitude of country quiet.

If one went to church, it was in best clothes (I once gloried in spring-sided boots) with gloves on, and carrying hymn-book and church service with brass-edged cover. The brass was apt to be scratchy at the corners. In winter, one was fortified for the coldness of the church with two cherries, brandy steeped, from a bottle of cherry brandy kept in the front-room cupboard. I never tasted them save on Sunday mornings. Entering church was a nervous

23

business. Did I not once walk in holding up an umbrella? "Litany Sunday" came every fourth week—a nuisance because I got stiff bending forward (I did not kneel) during the long Litany. The Athanasian Creed also lasted too long. I felt Jackson's *Te Deum* to be a grand thing. Sunday afternoon services—I by no means always was taken to those—were liable to tiresome interruptions from a baptism when one would have so much preferred to get on with the business and go home. The services seem to have left no impression save once only, when the curate spoke in his sermon about a mouse running about a church. That was worth hearing. It is likely enough that, less consciously, I was really deriving much profit from the decorous quiet of the church. The curate himself may have contributed to that effect; but an impression of it clings more to the name of another parson of that period—Mr Strange.

From the landing another stair-case—steep, narrow, crooked, dark—led to the top story—two rooms again. Of these the one in front was my Aunt Ann's room. Here you could peer down from the window into the street, getting a bird's-eye view of the tops of carts, waggons, cabs, and so on; but I didn't like this room. It is associated in my memories with ugly colours—veneered furniture, cheap red bed-hangings, and so on. Perhaps, as it was my Aunt's room (yet so far as I know she was never tiresomely prim) I did not feel quite free there to make a litter.

Not so in the back room, the "Attic." Was this a bedroom? I know it was my own bedroom afterwards; and as there was always a bed in it, it may have been in those earlier years a bedroom for the maid-servant who often acted as nursemaid to us small children. But the room was a play-room, and nothing else, for all I can tell to the contrary now.

At the very top of the crooked stairs was the first sign that this attic was the haunt of romping children; for here was a wicket gate to keep us, within, from tumbling downstairs. A step beyond, to the right, took one into the attic itself, and there——! There whatever was wanting in Aunt Ann's room opposite was more than made up for; for, there, one could be as untidy as one liked; could chatter, romp, play any games that came into one's head.

Whether there was or was not a fire-place; or if the lower window-sash ever opened, or where we kept our clothes, or what the chairs were, or the pictures (if any) or if the room boasted rug or a strip of carpet—these trumpery details have all quite gone from me. But a sort of air that the room had—an air of freedom for one's spirits as well as plentiful daylight—stays with me as a possession I shall not lose. Perhaps the daylight did it. The window faced north-west, so that the summer evenings grew very delicious there and (though that came a year or two later in my life) it was a treat, going to bed by sunset, to feel the dusk stealing through the familiar room as I fell asleep facing the sky and the earliest stars. At this window too, and in summer no doubt, I sometimes watched the rooks in Farnham Park; heard them cawing; liked the look of the park trees away there—a quarter of a mile off or so—standing up dark against the glow of the sky to the north.

Yet the attic was more properly a winter resort, and a very dear one, particularly at night when the curtains had been drawn and a candle lit. One candle we had, and that a tallow one. So we came to know about "shrouds," and "a thief in the candle" and so on, listening with a hushed feeling to the maid-servant's still-living folk lore. Sometimes the snuffers were missing from the tin candle-stick. Then the girl, at needlework, would use her scissors, and I for one felt nice and superior, because she called them "scithers." Sometimes—oh the joke!—the candle would be snuffed out and we were suddenly in the dark. But it didn't matter in company. Moreover there were curious odours to grow acquainted with—the smell of hot steel if the scissors had been used; or at any rate the smell of the smouldering tip of the candle-wick and of smoking tallow after a successful use of the snuffers.

Perhaps our usual pastime was to sit round the light, prattling over our various little jobs—my sisters at their needlework or doll-dressing, myself with a pair of scissors "cutting-out" figures for scrap-books. We sometimes played games. And if the games involved a little dressing-up, so much the better.

Such a game was the making and acting of a "dwarf," when one puts shoes on one's hands and so, standing behind a table but with apparent feet on it, and duly draped and veiled, looked very short indeed. Or there was "Dumb Dolly." This I liked very much indeed, if it fell to me to be the one to creep under the bed (this is how I know that there was a bed in the attic) and lie on my stomach in the dark, cocking my heels up from under the valance. When my heels had been dressed into a sort of a doll, how I loved to drop them forward or to shake them sideways, in "Yes" or "No" reply to the questioner! I don't recall any other games so rapturous; yet there must have been others. We searched for others often through a dilapidated book— *The Home Companion*—in which the wood-cuts were, possibly, by William Allingham. We might have got more games from this book, if we had been a larger family.

Other books included one I never liked—*The Little Lidgetts*—with bad type and an unpleasing page; a volume of two, almost equally unattractive, of *The Child's Companion*, and a thick dumpy volume named *Buds and Blossoms*. The worst of this little book was that some of its stories were so sad. When you came to "Far, far away, Little Peepy!" and knew that Little Peepy's parents were in India (wherever that might be) the cadences made you sob too much, and you read no more. Now and again a bound volume of *The Magnet Stories* turned up—'twas not so bad; and in the same mysterious way I sometimes came upon my old "Horn-book" as I called it. This—a little yellow card folded across the middle—gave the alphabet and a few short syllables (bab, cab, dab, and so on), and must have come into my experience very early, for I do not remember a time when I could not read it.

This "Horn-book" (who taught me that name for it?) was probably tumbled out when we took it into our heads to ransack the "Toy-box"—one of the treasures of the attic furniture. The toy-box, lined with spotted paper, held pell-mell, our broken toys—a wooden Punch short of arm or leg, a Jack-in-the-box, a monkey-up-a-stick from Farnham Fair perhaps, and last but not least, a real stuffed owl.

This poor dilapidated creature—so smooth—served all the purposes of a Teddy Bear.

To come back to books—Dr Watts's hymns, printed on untearable linen and disfigured with very inky wood-cuts, probably by Sir John Gilbert—was too obviously a book for infants and deserved no better place than the toy-box.

CHAPTER II

NEIGHBOURS

It seems like going back into ancient history to recall memories of any of the other folk of Farnham while I was a little child; and it is indeed likely enough that no such people, and no such dwellings or streets, are to be found any more in England. Railways had not yet had time to make much change; the pleasures, the business, of the place were those of the eighteenth century rather than of the twentieth; the townsfolk, with their old-fashioned behaviour, seem not to have travelled far in their outlook for centuries.

Next door to our newspaper shop, and now, like that, demolished for Mr Bentall's clothing establishment, was Bolland's shop for fruit and red herrings. A sash window, always thrown up, showed a slanting shop-front covered with boxes of fish and piles of apples and oranges and an unappetising and sticky heap of dates; while at the back would be seen old Mrs Bolland herself, in a red-and-blue woolly shawl which would have been the better for washing, it seems to me now. I don't know that I ever spoke to her, or went up the step into her shop. If our ball went over the palings into her back yard (narrower even than ours), it would be thrown back sooner or later.

On the other side of 18 Borough was "The Ship," less known even than Mrs Bolland's. Our own "Shutter-hole" intervened in front; at back our own shed screened off the back yard of "The Ship" altogether. From the street pavement a step *down* (not up as at Bolland's) gave access to a shut door beyond which I never saw; but, in our wash-house, on winter evenings, we could often hear the "clump-clump" of people dancing in the old public-house, or the rattle of a game of skittles. This low half-timbered building must have been a very ancient piece of Farnham. One morning my father, going out just before six o'clock to his business at the wheelwright's shop in East Street, found "The Ship" in ashes. It had been burnt to the ground during the night; yet none of us had heard anything of the fire.

Just opposite to us, across the street, was another old house and shop—toy-shop, and Post Office, up two or three steps, and kept by Miss Mary Nichols: a skinny little woman, very kind. Sometimes, if one of us children was unwell, she would lend us a toy from the shop, my sister says; an unbusiness-like act typical of the times, but I do not myself remember it. Soon after my memory begins, the Post Office was removed to a shop next door (a large place, I thought then) kept by Mr Robert Nichols. I watched the facia being lettered; it surprised me not to see "of us" for "Office." But, before that time, this place had been interesting to me for a scanty show of sponge cakes and other delights. For it was a confectioner's shop.

The confectioner's name, Burningham, was burnt into my memory by acute trouble. One morning my mother sent me across the street with "Mr Brummagem's Paper"; and I managed to repeat that name to the elderly man or woman behind the counter. Severe reproof correcting my pronunciation came swiftly. I fled back across the street, through our shop to the sitting-room behind; and there took refuge under the round table, in a burst of tears.

But this confectioner's shop had one other attraction. Below the shop window, and on a level with the iron-stone side-walk, was set a piece of green but not quite opaque glass, probably very thick and strong. This may have let in light to a cellar, but I don't know. What I do know is that once I saw a cock and several hens pass across behind that piece of glass. Once only. I never saw the apparition again, though I often looked for it. I did not know of any underground place there. Yet chickens passed.

Not so mysterious but equally rare was the sight, once only, of a monkey clambering about the front of "The Bush." Did he live there? I do not know. But I knew, and can still picture, a few human neighbours further along the street. In my mind I see a portly shoe-maker in a white apron come to his shop door. Then there is the green-grocer's shop, kept by a grim looking old lady and her two anxious-looking daughters. Round the corner of its counter was a forbidding pan of mouldy-looking stuff called "yeast." I shrank from the sight. A little farther along the street was a saddler's shop. The saddler's younger son wore surprisingly large boots, with tabs and laces very conspicuous to eyes so near to the pavement as mine. And behind the shop was a rope-walk. At least I once saw a man there walking backwards, in the process of twisting a rope.

With a little effort I can people the old street with its inhabitants—Tom Eyre the rubicund grocer, Charlie Bennett the machine-maker, Pullen the barber, Newman

31

the basket-maker, and many more; but of them all (in that direction) Tom Hackmen the fishmonger alone excites a truly pleasant memory. Mr Hackman—a man much esteemed by my father—had a shop facing Castle Street, where the Westminster Bank is now, and once I followed him into his back-garden (to think of it is like walking into some sunny garden of old Germany or old Holland) where he gave me—what I had never seen before—a tulip, all red and yellow. As I carried it gingerly home along the Borough, did not the ancient street glisten in the May forenoon with reflection of sunlight? Did not the canary in the shoe-shop doorway sing joyously, to see a tulip?

All this was along the Borough—"Up-street" as we used to say. But now, "Down-street," along East Street (past Bolland's) some other neighbours should be mentioned. First, across the road, in a place soon demolished to make way for South Street, lived Mr Williams. Mr Williams sold tea. In his window were two or three tall and dark images of Chinamen, which I should like to see again. Perhaps Mr Williams was also a general grocer: certainly the new wooden place to which he afterwards moved in South Street ("The New Road" we called it) was labelled, in big black letters, "Noah's Ark Grocery Stores." But the truly memorable thing about Mr Williams was the incurable huskiness of his voice. One could not be afraid of anybody who smiled so kindly; yet I never saw him without wonder, to hear a grown-up man talk in a whisper. I looked up at his face curious to hear; and the whisper always came—due to some disorder still unknown to me.

Just beyond Mr Williams's shop was a large gateway—where now one enters South Street—into The Bush Meadows, and just here too the main street of the old town widened out a little. For from the opposite side Bear Lane came into it here, as it does now, and just beyond Bear Lane three or four houses even as now (for they have not been pulled down) stood back so as to leave a shallow triangle in the street. Of these houses the one at the corner —"Queen Street Tavern" by official name—was known as "The Fourteenpenny House," I have often wondered why. Next to it was a corn merchant's shop—a queer old-fashioned shop up two or three steps—where dwelt my brother's school friend Charlie Ivens. I wonder if he is still living. The shop had a pleasant dry smell. Different kinds of cereals—heaps, bushels—lay in separate bins round the shop. The woodwork was dusty, or had been polished by emptying corn into the bins, until it had a rather shiny yellow colour.

Of Charlie Ivens himself more will have to be said; but I must tell how I once saw his father in very singular circumstances. Charlie took me into his house—front room, downstairs—and showed me his father lying in a stupor on the floor, behind a screen, the room being otherwise empty. It satisfied my childish curiosity to be told that Mr Ivens had small-pox. I thought no more about it. Not until lately did I hear how my mother was frightened, when she was told where I had been.

A few doors farther down East Street, past old Seymour's the hawker's, who was to be admired because he bought some of his fowls from Farnborough and possibly from my mother's beloved farm home there—a few doors farther down was another tavern, "The Unicorn," now disappeared, where dwelt, with his uncle the landlord, a school-fellow of my brother's. I looked up to this boy, chiefly, it would seem, for what I felt to be so clever in him—a folk-saying, none the worse for being admittedly picked-up from the landlord himself. According to this saying, a man need never be in difficulties if he had in his pocket a shilling, a knife, and a bit of string. So this slim boy was reported to have said, and to my admiring eyes he looked as if he was wiser than other boys.

Again a little farther on, and past yet another tavern—"The Green Man" this time, one of Farnham's many dismal public-houses—and on the same side—that is the north side of East Street, a yard gave way into a bakehouse. The street has been altered, just here, beyond recognition; nor can my memory recover at all a clear picture of the antique buildings; yet here, it is very certain, I went one Sunday to fetch home a hot dinner that had been cooked at the bakehouse. Less certainly, the cakes we had on Sundays only were also baked here, and had to be fetched away sometimes. This dim memory is perhaps reconstructed to account for a fairly fragrant memory of a nice cakey smell; yet—did I not indeed occasionally go to the old bakehouse on Saturday afternoon, to come away better provided for Sunday morning?

So far, I have told of nothing much more than a hundred yards away from my own home. I could get to the bakehouse without leaving the pavement. This pavement, by the way, as throughout the town, was of thin ironstones—

a little larger than a cigarette case—set in edgewise. The side walks thus paved were tolerably clean and dry, though not without shallow puddles in rainy weather, and for years I thought people fussy who complained that the stones hurt their corns. As a child I believed in no such inconvenience.

Across the street, where South Street was soon to be opened, a narrow door in the high wide gates let you into a footpath at back of the town—a footpath across "The Bush Meadows" to the railway station. But although, with a little effort, I might perhaps recall to memory the people who came next in the ancient street, not one of them is conspicuous there as a "neighbour." A very fat woman, proprietress of a butcher's shop, seems to have looked offensively fat to my childish fancy: a stately gentleman a little further on kept the Savings Bank and looked alarmingly dignified. But it is not until the schools are reached—Mr Poppleton's and my first school, Miss May's a little farther along the street—that memory grows alert again. And these schools must be left to a chapter by themselves.

CHAPTER III

THE PARK

FARNHAM PARK has quite a large share in the memories of my childhood. A biggish place—three miles round, so they used to say—for children it made a fine grassy play-ground, shady with trees, dignified with one long avenue (the "Lanes," my father said it had been called in his childhood) of old and tall elms. Sweeping slopes of grass, with plentiful trees, were the Park's main feature; five or six hollows or "dells"—disused and grass-grown chalk-pits or clay-pits—dimpled the sunshine of its wide slanting surfaces; patches of brake-fern made a secluded yet airy cover for the bishop's fallow deer; like a besieging foe regiments of stinging nettles stood here and there in the Castle moat; there were many different kinds and "clumps" of trees—oak and ash and thorn, beech, elm, lime, service, chestnut. To throw amongst the horse chestnuts stick or stone so as to bring down the glossy nuts was an adventure of breathless interest, though I myself was hardly brave enough for it, eager as I was to scamper away before being caught by "The Keeper," who was seldom seen, in fact. He was, to naughty little boys, a sort of conscience, named Hafacree.

The remoter corners of the Park—those solitudes, wild and romantic, that sloped up towards Hale and gave glimpses over half Surrey—these were seldom if ever visited until later years; nor were the ponds; nor was the tiny stream with its mysterious swallow-holes. All these

attractions lay waiting to be explored when I was bigger.
Time was not yet when I lay on a sloping bank under an
oak and watched the line of deer trip down to the stream
for an evening drink, and grew familiar with their coughing
to one another or with the twinkling of their tails. I had
not yet found, in one of the swallow-holes, a dead deer, or
hunted in the stream for caddis cases, or caught the glint
of a king-fisher flitting in and out of the tree shadows along
the winding sunlit stream bank. I had not seen ice on the
ponds, or discovered mistletoe in the stunted thorn-bushes
on the far off slopes. This was to come—all this; with
feelings as if Robin Hood might be under the next oak;
or with sound of wood pigeons in the elms, or sight of
squirrels or murmur of summer flies far up amongst the
tree branches—"Midsummer 'um," as a man said when
I invited him to hearken to it. These delights were for
later years. As yet, in my earlier childhood, it was enough
to have the vast expanse of glamour at my back door, so to
speak. For the Park was not so very far from 18 Borough.
From our attic bedroom we could see the nearer trees,
could sometimes hear the wind roaring through them;
could see, could hear, the rooks cawing homewards like
the very voice of quiet summer evenings. It all seemed
near, for outside our shop door, just round the corner,
was Bear Lane, leading gently up to the Stile, some two
or three hundred yards away.

How often in warm and golden weather we brothers and
sisters have straggled up that lane—a little party of children going to play in the Park.

In the very corner of the Park was "The Stile"—the

only practicable stile for us. Three other stiles there were indeed—one at each of the other three corners of the Park, to say nothing of the one near The Pound up beyond the Castle; but these others we seldom saw—they must have been half to three-quarters of a mile away if not more. The others moreover did not matter to us. Our stile—*The* Stile par excellence—led us immediately into our paradise, enclosed by the palings. Five or six wide oak steps up, a narrow sill, then three steps down the other side—there was only that delightful clamber between us and bliss. Substantial hand-rails to the stile had received letterings from many pocket knives and had grown dark brown with years of weather and of hand-clutchings, and the treads too were dark and worn. For hither converged many public foot-ways across the Park—from Hoghatch, from Hungry Hill, from Hale—for Farnham town; and it was not only children like ourselves who used that stile; but town loiterers and tradesfolk out for a walk, and labourers going to and from their work. Besides our little soft "puddies," the hardened palms of grown-up people—sawyers, hopground diggers, carpenters, brick-makers and bricklayers, to specify but a few—had helped to make those hand-rails all dark and shiny.

And here—though I really want to get over into the Park—I must linger long enough to recall my first introduction to ethnology. At the foot of the stile we had seen —my brother and I, aged ten and six perhaps—a gaunt and skinny labouring man, with leather gaiters that made his feet conspicuous, approach the stile to go over it, possibly for Hale. "A Saxon," whispered my brother.

How did he know? By the man's long, thin feet. That was
a sure sign. My brother may have been (he suggests now)
pulling my leg, but for years I believed this that he had
told me, and sometimes I thrilled at sight of "a Saxon,"
betrayed by his feet. Race differences were obviously
realities! I discerned that, at the foot of the stile.

Once over the stile, one felt one's-self to be "in the
Park," freer than before to scamper and enjoy life. The Park
lay tilted up before one's eyes—lower then, and seeing distances larger therefore—a vast spread of grass-land skirted
by tall trees in far-flung belts that met just at that corner.
There, to be sure, within the stile, the tread of wayfarers
had worn away all the grass down to the bare soil. But
farther on between the green tree-stems, one could see
the billowy uplands with cattle and horses browsing. The
elm avenue stretched far out of sight along the highest
ridge; "clumps" of trees dotted about here and there
showed up large distances; "The Big Dell," tree-crested
and lined all down its slopes as if with narrow sheep-tracks,
opened its hollow far up in the turf on the hither side of
the avenue. The Dell looked like a Colosseum to seat
thousands of people in the full sun there. Just within the
stile, however, one passed into the shade of tall trees where
rooks built, only too noticeably at certain seasons. Too
noticeably the bare ground was spattered with their drop-
pings; and once—it was Palm Sunday—my new jacket got
spattered too; and I wish I could remember now exactly
what was said at the time. That this misfortune was a
judgment on me I know: but what was it for? Was it for
not having a whole new suit, or can it have been for having

even so much new as a jacket on that day? Anyhow, there was luck, good or perhaps bad, in wearing new things on Palm Sunday. Those rooks, cawing overhead, proved it before I had walked three yards in the Park that day.

But whither should one go? That was the next question. Up the steep, straight in front of us? At the crest of that acclivity one would find, if one could not quite see from the stile, the low grey wall surrounding Farnham Castle. Low it was, for a dry moat further protected the castle from the outside—so low that at one part of the wall could be just seen the top of a lean-to greenhouse against it in the bishop's garden within. And the wall was a cool grey, because it was built of roughly squared boulders. I knew those boulders pretty well. From the mortar between them dropped plentiful ivy-leaved toad-flax; and, better than the toad-flax to my partial eyes, large fronds of wall-rue fern and of wall-spleenwort hung down. Violets grew at the foot of the wall—white violets, probably strays from the garden within, or may be from the "rubbish heap" pitched over the wall into the plentiful waste room of the moat. A touch of mystery was added to the moat by a low door half-way down from the Park. This door was kept locked: it led to "the ice-house" I learnt, though I hardly learnt what that meant. Outside the moat opposite a shut gateway in the wall, "The Avenue" began—began with two huge elms. Passing into that end, one looked down a vista of half or three quarters of a mile of tall trees in two straight lines, that met overhead, stately as a cathedral aisle. But before the moat gave way to the avenue the soil rose into a mound that must have been dumped all round when the moat was dug out in prehistoric ages. And along this mound ran the path one had ascended from the stile. Here, too (missing the avenue), one came out into sunshine; but all the way up from the stile had been shady under high trees.

All the length of the Avenue was fairly level. If you walked along it away from the Castle and could take your eyes from the shimmering maze of branches that now and then gave peeps of cloud or blue—tiny flecks and points of sky—you might be rewarded by all sorts of lovely landscape. On your left (northwards) where the wilder stretches of Park still sloped upwards towards Hale, you were pretty sure to see horses here and there; and in the patches of fern amongst the clusters of trees, fallow-deer. By the way— and this seemed mysterious to us children—the deer rarely appeared on the other side of the Avenue. If they did cross to that side it was said to be a sign of rain. And sure enough, in after years, if ever I did see the deer south of the Avenue, the day was wet. What was the explanation? Were the deer in league with the Clerk of the Weather? Had they some secret inspiration, unknown to human beings? Why did they never cross the Avenue, unless it rained? That was a puzzle to my childish mind. And it was still a puzzle long after I had realised that the Avenue (perhaps marking a prehistoric track) lay along a ridge near where the chalk formation began. It seemed unlikely even when I learnt that much that the deer would care greatly whether their feeding-place should or should not be rain-soaked. And in my childhood I knew little about chalky soil. I only knew that the deer seemed mysteriously to avoid that side of the Avenue in the warm sunny weather that drew human beings to it. It took me years to comprehend that probably one thing explained the other. At any rate it was the fact that the deer kept away in the wilder parts of the park whenever there were people who might have disturbed them nearer the town, that is to say on fine summer days.

Going eastwards along the Avenue from the Castle, if you looked between the elm trees—one after another—on your right instead of on your left, it was towards East Street and Guildford Road that you looked—but they lay a long distance down in the hollow. There were the hop-gardens to hide the back of the old street, if nothing else; but not much even of the hop-gardens could be seen from the Avenue in the Park. At the foot of the wide grassy slope the very stile, with the cleft-oak paling beginning from it, was shut out from sight under the continuous belt of trees already mentioned. Consider again the position of this belt. About half way between high road and avenue it stretched along for nearly a mile, a parallelogram on either hand. That to the south, outside the fence, was filled full-up with hop-grounds, slanting down towards the public road. But the parallelogram on the north side, within the Park itself, and continuing the rise from the town, was a delicious grass-slope—dotted with tree clumps here and there—reaching up to the Avenue. Here, on this grass-slope deer browsed in wet weather; but here children played, on warm summer days.

At some far-off time the slope had been under the plough. From Avenue down to park-paling the turf still showed

the ancient "Lands"; while now and again a decrepit
thorn on a low bank seemed the relic of a forgotten hedge-
row. But forgotten indeed it all was, when I was a little
child at play there. I noticed, rather, the turfy mole-hills,
the cow-pats sometimes covered by brown dung-flies that
whirred up as you passed, the dells, but always and everywhere the thick velvet of grass.

I think this turf was the real fascination of the whole
place. The shade of the tree clumps was delicious: sometimes we had an impromptu pic-nic there, my mother's
maid-servant bringing out to us tea in a jug wrapped in a
blanket to keep it warm. Those were golden summer afternoons indeed. And sometimes perhaps we were impressed
by the glimpses to be caught here and there of the reposeful
country—the woods, the fields, the white dusty roads—
away to the south of old Farnham. Yet, if these things did
indeed impress us, their influence must have been shed on
us unawares; for we were too young then to care much for
the loveliness of that quiet distance, though we may have
felt its peace. But we were not too young to delight in the
grass. The grass—acres, miles, of it—was always there,
and always a source of sheer bliss.

It was a green and clean playground, with room in it
for thousands. We sprawled on it as on a cushiony bed;
sat down on it when and where we chose; rolled over and
over, down its hollows, in jolly laughing safety. And it
allowed us to get very near to the soil—nearer than is
possible in age—as we lay on our faces, peering into the
thickest sward and watching the struggling progress of
this or that small insect. Dry scents came up to us from

43

last year's decaying grasses, from the little crumbling clods of the earth itself.

Now and again a green-covered heap tripped up the unwary. Was it originally a mole-heap, or had it been begun as well as ended by ants? If kicked, it would send out regiments of tiny red-brown "emmets," hurrying and disturbed. I did not molest them often—perhaps disliking, myself, to see them so put about. But those hillocks made no real difference. On them, as everywhere, the turf had been browsed down short, save only at one season. At one summer season the grass growing too fast for the quiet sheep, deer, cattle, covered itself, to our great satisfaction, in acres and acres of its own browny trembling blossom—our beloved and admired "totter-grass." How beautiful and graceful it was! We saw that, gloating over the gracefulness of the single spires as we gathered them, yet not prevented thereby from picking tight ugly handfuls. Was it for little or no purpose? What else should a child do with flowering grass? We took the handfuls home: got them set in vases on the piano for winter decoration! They must have grown as dusty as they were ugly: if they added one more to my mother's too abundant house-keeping cares I should not wonder; but still less should I wonder (though I have no real recollection of such a thing) to learn that those same unlovely and dusty bunches of grass were enriched for us children by many and many an association with romps in the Park in hot weather. Hot summer weather, when down in the short turf, one found little low-growing flowers—tormentils, and especially, lady's slippers orange tawny and dainty. Remembrance of these jumps into my mind now. Not much else. By trying, I get (but I have to try for it) pictures of little flimsy blossoms of white clover. Memory too recovers tiny brooms (like fairy brooms) my sisters made, binding one grass stem round a score or so of stems of other grasses—not totter grass, which was too spreading. In the same store-house of memory I find heads of wild barley, strangely creeping up into the armholes of my little waistcoat. So far they had climbed up, having been put inside the wristbands of my jacket sleeves for that very purpose.

What we played at I cannot at all remember; but I do remember getting very hot at it. And I dimly remember getting home in the warm evenings and going down into a cool dim cellar to get "cream of tartar" water my mother had made for us. The dim light, the cool air—what a delicious preparation for bed-time! One home-going to be sure, is not quite so dim. Hot (it was a glowing summer evening) I was running down Bear Lane, perhaps half blinded by sweat. At any rate I did not see—and indeed never thought of since until now I wonder what became of him—a still smaller urchin with a toy wheel-barrow, over whom I fell headlong, all asprawl on my face. How I roared! The next in my memory is the interior of a shed in Ivens's yard, where a Good Samaritan was saying "That's where *you* laid last!" Who was he? "The head cook and bottle washer," Charlie Ivens said; and for years afterwards I held that to be his occupation. Anyhow he rinsed my hands for me; and supplied me too with a useful word—gravel-rash. Gravel-rash, I understood, was very hot and smarting, all across the palms of both hands.

CHAPTER IV

SCHOOLS

I don't remember learning to read. The little folded card or "horn-book" already mentioned, it is true, had no longer than three-lettered words, but I could always read them. So far as I know to the contrary I was born with that power.

But this did not excuse me from going to school; and even on my very first afternoon at Miss May's I learnt something. I had been told to write, on a slate, the numbers to a hundred. Easy! And I got on capitally up to 20; but 21 proved my downfall. If twenty was "two nought," of course twenty-one was the same with "one" after it— "two nought one." So I reasoned, and so I wrote: 20, 201. But somehow it would not do, and I had to write again all the numbers from twenty to a hundred; missing so the play I might have had with some cowrie shells.

This was almost my first lesson at Miss May's, and I never forgot it. Nor do I forget how troublesome it was, there, to trace pot-hooks and hangers in Darnell's copy-book. Perhaps—though it never occurred to me until now —my dislike of this task was due partly to the room to which we adjourned for it: a downstairs back-room (facing to the north) with never any sunshine in it at the hour while I was there. Most of the schooling went on in sunny front rooms and I did not dislike it; but at this writing I grew unhappy.

In my first weeks or months we went to the top of the

house three stories up. (The house is still there—a barber's shop now.) From the windows we could see over the opposite low houses to "The Broad Meadows" and to Crooksbury Hill in the distance. Sometimes mist clung round that Hill; and at such times, my brother taught me, Crooksbury was said to be "in his night-cap." I took it in, seriously. It was a thing as important to know as that twice two are four.

One afternoon I clambered up the stairs when the rest of the school was already busy. I cannot think, now, why I was myself late. But it seems I was determined to make a half holiday of it. When Miss May asked if I was not proposing to stay, I assured her that I had got to go home; and when, at home again, I was questioned if Miss May did not ask me to stay, I said "No." Well, she didn't— exactly. But it was a near thing for my conscience. The quibble was somehow not quite satisfying, though successful. I only remember playing truant one other time, as told elsewhere.

Truly school was rather pleasant. There it was, to be sure, that I was broken of my habit of drawing with my left hand. But at least I drew. I drew fancy mountains, as spiky as anything, but right enough, according to the boy next me. Unfortunately none of these drawings are left. They were done on my slate—a sort of thing unknown to modern children, who have to scribble on paper.

And if my school pastimes (and tasks too, very likely) were pleasant, my little companions were interesting—or some of them were. There was, especially, a Scotch boy named Colin. He had a terrible big brother at the

47

Grammar School; and Colin himself had an air—fine, boastful, manly, swaggering. The awe with which I heard of his brother's greatness made me also a little afraid of Colin himself. He, for his part, was afraid of nothing. So he would have said, and perhaps did say. (Poor fellow, when last I heard of him, he had emigrated to America and died of consumption.)

I looked upon him, therefore, with admiration, by no means seeking to emulate him. When, leaving the school-room of an afternoon at the same time with me, he crawled down the first flight of stairs head foremost, I knew I was not brave enough to do that. My part was to look on, and wonder. So I never ventured to dispute with him when he teased me. "Two jolly Englishmen," he said,

Two jolly Englishmen and one Portuguee—
One bonny Scotchman could fight all three.

I may have had some doubt on this point; but it did not occur to me to put the question to the test in person. Indeed, I should have been afraid to do so. Colin was perhaps no bigger than myself, but of fiery and determined mien, as became the brave.

Another boy—a tinsmith's son—took my fancy so well that I tried stealing slate pencils for him. I knew the drawer where they were kept in our shop, and tiptoed round the counter to it several times before I was caught and my generosity stopped. A bigger boy (my brother's friend, rather than my own—for I felt too respectful to presume to friendship for a year or two with one so aged) cautioned me that this was not quite an intimacy to be desired. But not before the tinman's son had invited me to share a treat

48

with him. He was going to see a bullock killed: would I join him? Rather! If my mother would permit. I was unlucky enough to ask her, and felt aggrieved because she would not let me go. And the upshot of it is that here I am far past the prime of life, and have not yet seen a bullock killed, or anything else bigger than a cat.

Not the faintest recollection of this boy in school remains with me; yet, now I come to think it over, he is not singular in that. Colin remains: a class or two—a semi-circle or two—in which I seem to be standing up with other boys and several biggish girls—this also is in my memory, where for the rest, little else of that old school is left save dim pleasant "atmospheres." The daylight looks agreeable; shadowy people, happy enough, congregate in quiet reflected sunlight; there is a vague sense that tables and book-filled cupboards are in the room; but the individual people I cannot see.

Excepting Miss May herself. She, small, already wrinkled and worn-looking—wearing plentiful dark clothes, flimsy of texture, beady, lacy—Miss May, so thin, so fragile, so inoffensive, is not yet effaced from my memory. She is gentleness and kindness embodied. Once she lifted me, sobbing bitterly over some forgotten trouble, on to her lap and comforted me as my mother would have done; and my memories of her are worth keeping fresh. I don't recall much about her school; but I am thankful to her for making it a happy place for a little child to be in.

For all that, I did not dislike staying away sometimes.

49

I had a little white gathering on one finger—a thing to be proud of in itself; and the finger had to be poulticed with a bread poultice and afterwards bound up with rags into a "dolly." It was not really bad; but it gave good excuse for staying away from school that afternoon. And then—who so gratified as I?—my mother put on her walking things and took me with her on some unknown errand of her own—perhaps to find some sick newspaper boy or maidservant. Whatever the errand, it got a sort of afternoon calm into it; perhaps because it was an unwonted thing for my mother to be out walking at all, but likelier because of her own habitual manner.

Our way took us across Farnham, down Downing Street, and round two corners to Longbridge. There the Wey—"The River" as it is still called—widens out into a ford while the street crosses it in a bridge; and there we stopped. For there down by the ford, a boy was trying to drown a half-grown cat. We saw him throw the thing into the water, then saw it swim back to the river-bank, only to be picked up and thrown in again. But after we had watched this performance two or three times my mother could bear it no longer. She explained to the boy how to do his job quickly and therefore mercifully. He was to put the cat into a pail half full of water and then inserting another pail hold the cat down into the water until it was dead, which would not be more than a minute or two. I suppose then we hurried away, for I remember no more at all. Many years afterwards, acting on my mother's advice to that boy, I was able myself to destroy a pet that had to be killed; so I know it was good advice. But was it taken that afternoon? I am recalling only that it was not uncommon at that period to see a drowned cat or dog in "The River." The town drainage was not to come for many years. In this particular case I do not know what happened; or whether my mother and I went farther; or if anything more was done about the gathering on my finger. My memory is a complete blank as to the whole expedition. But at least I had a half holiday from school, and thought a gathering on my finger rather an important thing and did not disapprove of wearing a bread poultice.

But why or in what circumstances I left Miss May's and found myself eventually going to Mr Poppleton's I have not the least idea.

Here—for I fancy it goes back to this happy almost infant time—patches of clean morning sunshine splash across my memory, in connection with the china shop a few doors farther up the street. Here dwelt that elderly schoolfellow of my brother's who had gravely cautioned me against the tinsmith's son, and with whom I was one day, in school, to speak of the Tichbourne Trial; here in one window of his father's shop, were displayed every summer the prizes for the coming "Athletic Sports"; and naturally the probable winners of them had to be talked over, or shouted over, as is the way with little boys. Other such heroes were not even dreamt of as these stalwart long-jumpers, high-jumpers, runners in the hundred yards race, the mile race—fellows of twenty, perhaps; and there, glistening in the shop window, swathed in velvet, were the sacred silver things they were to win. Probably the window had had an extra rub, to make it shine the more; yet the summer morning was probably dry if not sunny, or I should not have been looking in. Next door was the shop yard; and at least once I stood in the doorway of a loft there, looking down on to a heap of sunlit yellow straw, where a cart load of crockery was being unpacked.

CHAPTER V

SQUIB-NIGHT

TOWARDS dusk on the afternoon of the fifth of November every year the quiet streets of Farnham—quiet as with an eighteenth century sleep—used to echo from end to end with sounds of hammering. The townsfolk were nailing up barricades over their windows. Not over shop windows, indeed. Shops were anyhow shuttered and barred every night, and needed no special protection against the celebrations of Gunpowder Treason. But the windows of all living-rooms facing the street on the ground floor (and every townsman then lived in the town) had to be boarded over lest some squib should bang through. For like reasons sacks were stuffed close up under cellar gratings in the pavements, to keep out the plentiful sparks and explosions of the coming night. It was only the lower windows that had to be guarded. Those on the first floor were left, perhaps with some risk. The risk was lest a squib should "rise," as it was said to be sure to do if spirits of wine had been used in making it. A rising squib was, to be sure, dangerous. I remember seeing the round hole in a glass fanlight, through which a squib had rushed the night before. Perhaps a squib could go clear over a house. At any rate my father was wont, on those nights, to walk out to the back yard last thing and satisfy himself that all was right in the lofts. Perhaps his chief object was to soothe my mother, but it may well have been a time of anxiety for any householder. Earlier in the evening he had walked "down"

East Street to see that his wheelwright's shop was not on fire.

Truly, precautions were needful. The old town went mad. Lewes, they used to say, was if possible wilder in its Guy Fawkes celebrations, but otherwise in all the South of England there was no other town ran riot, that night, so wantonly, so recklessly, as Farnham did. At least we were proud to think so. A true mediaeval day, or night rather, survived in that pandemonium, when one heard squibs hissing, spluttering, banging almost incessantly—now here, now there; when strange figures in disguise flitted about the dark streets and lanes, and sudden explosions of sparks showed unsuspected groups lurking in shadowy corners.

Bonfires were lit in the main street—two if not more— one at the foot of Castle Street, the other opposite the opening of Bear Lane. There were probably others. For there was no motor traffic then to obtain decorum from all else on the roads; nor were there any "swells" abroad in Farnham that night to demand it. The vulgar, the populace, had it all their own way. And they went afoot. If a stray cart or waggon from afar wanted to pass through the town—bound perhaps for Guildford, or for Winchester, that was a most unusual interruption. Not more than once or twice in an evening would it happen. The only thing to be expected was the passing of the Mail Cart from Farnborough at about nine o'clock or so. To let that go by the bonfire was raked aside, and then at once raked back into the street again for the revelry and noise to go on.

So at least I heard. I was to be sure much too small to be allowed out alone after dusk; and certainly I should have been scared out of my wits. Yet I knew some things by direct observation. I recall now how the squibs began as night fell on the dark town where no street lamps were lit. Now we would hear a loud bang close at hand: "A whopper," we laughed, "by the Bush Gateway!" Immediately it was answered from a distance. "West Street," we surmised, or "Downing Street," as the case might be. Now and again a cracker on the pavement made a diversion: now and again we saw a Catherine wheel ("Catten-wheel") whirl its hissing sparkles round and round. A rocket would go up with a roar: one hoped its stick would not fall on any inflammable stuff in one's back yard. And once a "guy" stood at the foot of Bear Lane firing the brilliant globes of a "Roman Candle" up the lane past the very Police Station. But for the most part the squibs were home-made. For weeks beforehand boys were spending their leisure at that preparation—a sort of wicked cookery in which gunpowder, iron-filings, saltpetre, and touch-paper were the well-known ingredients boys discussed with one another. On the appointed night the products of this manufacture were slung round waist or neck in a bag or a tin canister, for the "guy" wearing it to get at easily in the dark. But too often sheer carelessness over this led to an accident, and next morning the town was shocked to hear how "young So and So" had been burnt by having his squibs afire round his waist. Yet these mishaps had to be taken as part of the game. If one was old enough, yet not too old and nowise too staid, the thing to do on the Fifth of November was to dress up as a "guy" and prowl about the dark old streets with squibs.

A "guy" probably wore a mask, and was covered fantastically in plenty of paper shavings (to dangle wantonly like scalps) and white or shiny paper, to show up suddenly if a squib was thrown down near one. A certain "guy" (one of my mother's newspaper boys) came out of the dark street one night into the little dim shop and near the gas-jet, where he could be seen. Then, to my great admiration, suddenly the first boy was gone and another stood in his place! So, to my astonished eyes, it seemed for a moment or two, until I understood that the boy's back had a different scheme of disguise from the front. A well-equipped "guy" carried either a switch, or a holder for putting down his squibs far enough away. For it was not well to be too close to a burning squib: the wretched thing would follow in the draught made by running away from it. Spluttering and roaring out its stream of sparks, it would chase after any runner, as if with malice for a few yards, throwing his scampering figure into strong light, and then bursting as if in devilish hatred. Now and then you would see a little crowd suddenly scatter from some screaming squib stealthily lit amongst them. A rush, a hiss, a bang, and then darkness—it made us children laugh, in the safety of an upstairs room.

The procession of the Guy Fawkes to the bonfire was dreadful to behold. Consider. For some hours we children had stood at the window in the dark Front Room, doubtless exciting one another over all the weird happenings down in the street. There the familiar buildings were but fitfully lit up by glare of torches, or frequent explosions. Odd figures flitted along for a moment, only to be lost

again in the November darkness. In this or that doorway
or passage, usually so ordinary, so safe, some fearful miscreant could be seen lurking as if for crime; across the
road where one had skipped and scampered light-heartedly,
now, in this darkness and orgy, uncanny men were stealing
quickly by in the gleam of squibs or of bonfires. Of course
we were excited, probably talked gaspily, had seconds of
listening stillness, then were startled by hiss and bang.
And in a thrill of expectation we went downstairs to supper,
for the great affair of the night was yet to come. So we
munched our bread and cheese supper under the gas-jets
of the little back room, laughing belike at this or that
crackling bang out in the street. And by and by, from
a distance—probably far "up" West Street—a different
sound just took our attention. Hark! Was it the band?
Surely that was it!

> I'm ninety-five and I'm ninety-five,
> And to keep single I contrive.

Soon all doubt ended. The local Volunteer Band (one
"Lapper" May great amongst them) were escorting Guy
Fawkes to the bonfire and soon the procession would be
passing our window!

No more thought of supper, then! We raced back upstairs, into the Front Room that was aflicker from the doings
in the street and took up our places at the window to see
the Guy Fawkes go by.

And as it drew nearer and the band brayed louder, the
hurly-burly increased. There were more guys about, more
squibs, until at last, with the procession itself, came a perfect uproar of fiendish riot: noise, flaming torches, screeching

squibs, dreadful looking men, and—horridest of all—a
Guy Fawkes, or maybe two of them—ferocious though
motionless figures, wearing masks, black hats, black coats.
The very motionlessness of them was fearsome. They
looked like dead men. Their hideous faces, with too much
red about them, gleamed and glowed like a butcher's shop
lit by naphtha flares; and for the rest the straw they were
stuffed with, the tar they were darkened with, made them
too inflammably black. A hell of pitchy blackness hung
over the figures of Guy Fawkes. And around them howled
lurid madmen in disguise; squibs roared and banged; a bit
of old England had indeed come yelling back to life in the
November night along the unlighted old-world street.

Yet I hardly saw the procession before, overcome with
terror, I had crouched down behind the lower panelling of
the window until one could dare look out again. What
made it worse was—and yet the fact was a little re-
assuring too—that the procession halted for a moment
just below our window—the window in my father's little
house—for some extra demonstration, some louder band-
playing or special cheering. Indeed it was comforting to
know that this was for my father's benefit. For, be it
explained, the Guy Fawkeses amidst their gang of demons
were being drawn along on a goods-delivery van. Mason
had lent the van, so no doubt he was cheered, too. But it
had fallen to my father in his wheelwright's shop to floor
the van over with a boarded platform; and as he had doubtless done this gratuitously, he now had to be thanked. But
his work (little as he guessed it) had actually added to my
fright. Thanks to the platform, the figures—bloody-faced

Guy Fawkeses, guys with their sputtering squibs, trumpeting and drumming bandsmen, and all, were almost on our level at the window, and so much the more dreadful to cause one to shrink and shudder down out of sight. Happily they soon passed on to the bonfire just round the corner at the foot of Bear Lane. After that—well, then I suppose we went to bed; for I remember no more about Squib-Night. One comes next to the following morning, with the streets littered with empty squib cases, and reeking with the smell of burnt powder, while a grey winter quiet hangs over the old houses, rather melancholy.

CHAPTER VI

AT GRANDFATHER'S

ABOUT a furlong away, and on the same side of the street as 18 Borough, was "The Shop," that is to say my father's Wheelwright Shop, in the house adjoining which lived his father, my own grandfather, George Sturt. One advantage of being on that northern side of the street was that at both places we got the sunshine in at our front doors, and very good it was to see that warm light on the wheelwright's floor, yellowish and quiet and soft over the litter of chips and shavings. But a greater advantage was that, no change of roadside being involved, it was quite possible for me to toddle off by myself to my grandfather's, as soon as I was able to toddle at all. It wouldn't be safe for a little child now; but in those quieter sleepier times there was nothing to fear, and I did it often. At what age I began to go alone cannot be remembered. I must have been used to the walk before I was four years old; for I recall starting off, on the morning of my fourth birthday, to show to my grandfather my birthday present: a Mavor's Spelling Book.

At the wheelwright's shop itself sundry small mishaps befell me, the place being to us privileged children a sort of playground. We jumped across the sawpit, swung round and round on the handle of the big grindstone, muddled about with the dirty water of the shoeing-hole, clambered on to the five-bar gate shutting off the hop-ground at the top of the lane outside (where South View and

St Cross begin now). I used to sit on the top rail of that gate, exulting to be there. And once, flinging my legs over from the gate-post into the adjacent cottage-garden, I was able to look down gloriously upon the cabbages or potatoes. But presently, recklessly forgetting, I slipped off from my perch to the wrong side of the wall, into the garden—and I must have been very small, to be so scared. "Old Jack" (a harsh-voiced old woman who went by that name) might come out from the cottage and catch me, in her garden! A braver, or a larger, boy would have climbed the wall. It was about four feet high, built of flints and tarred, and its top rounded. But I couldn't climb it! With my heart in my mouth I ran along the path towards the cottage and let myself out by the side gate, heartily glad to be safe in the lane again, opposite my father's yard across the lane.

In front of the wheelwright's shop, against the street, carts and waggons for repair stood under the old elm, there not being at that time, before the South View yard was bought, any room for them elsewhere. And one afternoon, under the old elm tree, clambering about an empty cart (two-wheel, you know) that slanted forwards there with its shafts on the ground beside the street, I presently climbed up towards the tail end. How was I to know that empty carts might overbalance? But that is what this one did. Treacherously, before I had time to realise that I had made a mistake and weighed a little myself, the cart tipped. As if I was one of its loads it shot me towards the ground, and that is all I know excepting that I yelled loud and long.

Another time, near the same place, that is to say in front of the shop and against the street, I carelessly stepped "plop" into a paint-pot of red lead a man had set on the ground there. Memory doesn't tell me whether I yelled then or the man swore or if my mother was much vexed. The paint-pot—scarce five inches across—could only have been stepped into by a very small foot.

But there was another time when I yelled, and to this day a misshapen finger-nail shows why. I was hammering, and hammered my finger—and there still the nail grows crinkled. Moreover, being on my right hand, it proves that the hammer was in my left. And that reminds me that at Miss May's school I was broken of drawing on my slate with my left hand. The hammer taught me a similar lesson at the shop. Yet my left hand continued my best, until palsy overtook me, for sundry other actions; and a certain clumsiness that has ever hampered me with my right hand makes me dubious of the wisdom of correcting me at school. Still, it is a pity to be different from other people; and one or two left-handed men I have known have suffered so many inconveniences as to make one afraid to be dogmatic. Gaucherie is not exactly a new word and was never used in praise.

Just past the little office my father had had put up (it was built with double-boarded sides, the space between the boards being stuffed with sawdust), just past this tiny place was a back-door to my grandfather's. Indeed my memory recalls an earlier time, before the office was put up. At that far-off day, a step-ladder led up to a little loft, which had once been the "work-room" where my father's sister Margaret and her apprentices worked at their dress-making.

One childish memory clings to that cool shaded spot beside the step-ladder. For it was only there as far as I remember, though it must have been elsewhere, that I used to caper to and fro astride of Old Polly—the only horse I ever rode. I think Gargantua, in his childhood, had similar horses. To my grandfather Old Polly seemed an old walking-stick with flattened blobby head; but she always carried me as far as I wished, and as fast. A capital horse.

The front way, from East Street into my grandfather's house, was just past the wheelwright's shop, up under the elm tree, for shop and house stood on the same property and were, in fact, built into one another. A low wicket paling, painted white, enclosed the property and kept the things within—the carts in front of the shop and next them the house-garden—well away from the street a couple of feet below.

Looking back through the branches of the elm or past the huddle of carts in front of the wheelwright's shop, you saw the quiet provincial traffic—the countrified wayfarers and the occasional vehicles (horse-drawn in those days) and the dingy old street, grey at dusk or in rainy weather, but scintillating and fresh-looking on bright days. The house-door at Number 83 opened straight into the living room, no passage or hall or lobby intervening. There you were plump on the family. They might be at dinner, or my grandfather might be writing his ledger or he and my crippled Uncle John might be taking an afternoon nap each over a newspaper—it was all one. Anybody from the street had but to open the door and there the family was.

As I remember it, the room thus entered had a brick

floor, well sanded. Yet can it have been so? What I am sure of was the open hearth, at an angle across the inner corner farthest from the street door. On one side of this hearth my grandfather used to sit facing anybody coming in. Opposite to him, so as to be on the right hand of visitors or customers, sat always Uncle John. He was paralysed. Even with help he wanted a stick, and his walking-stick was always near him. Between these two men lay a hearth-rug—a rug made of small shreds of cloth (mostly black) strongly sewn on to canvas by their ends. Rugs of this sort never wore out. On this one I used to squat before the fire, looking up at my Grandfather and my Uncle. It must have been from them that I got my horse Old Polly—the walking-stick already mentioned; but my Grandfather was too busy to give much heed to me, and it was my Uncle John whom I chiefly remember in this connection. I like to think of his black hair and beard and his kind tired eyes, and his smile. Sometimes (as I have told in another place) he would be persuaded to poke his stick into the little heap of sawdust smouldering on the hearth, so as to send up the chimney the sudden rush of red sparks. I liked to see that! "Squibs!" I cried, thinking of squib-night. If Uncle John was reading the paper, then, I noticed, his lips were moving; he even whispered the very words, for himself of course, but by me audible.

My Grandfather never whispered loud enough to be heard though I fancy his lips moved. Too often for my pleasure, he sat writing at the table in the middle of the room, this being his only office; and if I shook the table it seemed to me absurd in him to be so touchy about it as to protest.

He would often hold his pen cross-wise between his gums (I think it was a "magnum bonum" or barrel pen, with shortish yellow stick) as he had no pen-rest for it though he had a pen-wiper. This of course was when he wanted both hands for turning over his ledger pages. Behind him was a glazed book-case—of my father's make, I afterwards learnt. What was in it? I remember only a volume with a crude engraving of a man looking very gloomy, and under it the legend "Johnson's Dictionary. Word 'Gaolbird.'" (As I read this legend, or heard it read, the second and third words were not divided by a stop, but were hyphenated.) It may have been in the same volume that my aunt sometimes found for me a picture of a waterfall— a very smooth-gushing and unimpeded fall, as if poured from a spout.

From this room a smaller one opened out, through a doorway just within the street door, there being in fact no other way into it. Thus secluded, and with a window in the front of the house, it made a more private yet a quite presentable retreat for my grandfather if his business should ever require such a thing; and it went by the name of "The Parlour." But I seldom entered it and remember little about it. It had a fire-grate, but never a fire in my recollection. Against the wall opposite the window stood a white-painted piece of cabinet work which was called "The bowfette." Behind its glazed doors gleamed glasses —many of them probably; two of which had names for me —"Old Tom" and "Young Tom"; but of them I must tell some other time.

If you went straight across from the street door without

turning into the sitting-room, you came to another door opposite, and this was the way into the kitchen. On two nails standing out from one beam hung a gun—"Your father's" Aunt Sarah told me. It didn't interest me or surprise me. Of course my father was able to shoot or to do anything else if he liked: I knew that well enough. But I had never known him to use a gun; and I did not, even then, see why anybody ever should.

Going on straight across the kitchen, you came to the back door, passing first (on your right) a pantry door; and next—just within the back door itself—a staircase door. I think the back door had a round towel on it. Beside the door (on the left-hand) came a long window, probably with lead lights; and then, at right angles, across the kitchen and opposite the pantry, a fireplace with open hearth.

Quiet light, yet not much, came to the hearth from the window with its north aspect. There may have been room for a chair or a narrow table under the window, but then at once came the sooty hollow of the fire-place. Cast-iron dogs were there, the fuel being waste cart-timber and blocks and chips from the wheelwright's shop and perhaps some sawdust. Within the black hollow of the hearth hung pots and kettles; and in front of it, hooked to the woodwork of the chimney-piece, hung down sometimes a ticking roasting-jack. I liked (without any thought that I can remember) to watch that jack and to hear it, so methodically turning the joint or the game before the fire. I liked to see my aunt basting the savoury dinner from the pan of almost boiling dripping underneath the roast. Most of all it rejoiced me, when she made a gridiron cake. How good it was to see the piece of pastry laid on the gridiron and so stood down over the glowing wood-ashes! How good to smell it cooking! And at last, what perfect bliss to have the very cake itself, black-barred from the gridiron, put into one's hands all hot, and so to set one's teeth into the crisp and flaky dainty!

And the making of the pies was a sight to watch. It was a sight to see Aunt Sarah, after rolling out a piece of pastry very thin, proceed to cover it with dabs from thumb or finger of salt butter and lard in alternate lines, first butter then lard; which had to be then worked and rolled into the pastry. At last a limp sheet of pastry was laid over the pie for a cover, and with a knife was trimmed round to the pie dish, the trimmings being folded together into a lump and rolled out again. Now was the chance, and sometimes it came off, to get a gridiron cake; but what became of the pies or where they were baked I haven't the faintest idea.

Generally my occupation in that kitchen was to sit and watch. Yet, when there was no cooking going on, we played—or perhaps it would be truer to say "had larks." "We." Somebody at any rate—probably my brother— shared with me the interest of one silly thing I seem to see us doing there. We each got a longish piece of the stem of a "churchwarden" pipe, holding it upright in our mouths. Into the top end was dropped a pin thrust through a holly berry; and by blowing steadily and lightly the holly berry and pin could be lifted up just far enough to dance about above the pipe-end without actually falling out; but if you gave too hard a puff, down came the pin, loaded with the berry, on to your upturned face. It hurt a little: but that may have been the essence of the game, for probably one thought it fun, and laughed.

Sometimes my grandfather would stand at the open back-door and begin his curious whistle—"phew-ioo-ioo-ioo-ioo." It was to call his pigeons. At once the birds came circling down on level wings—a stately sight: but there was nothing stately in their hurry to and fro bobbing their heads—bob-bob-coo-coo—to gobble up the peas tossed for them into the little brick courtyard. One of them one day got a foot jammed into a walnut shell, and went clattering about the courtyard wearing it like a boot; and we laughed to see it. The pigeons came down from one of the lofts at the wheelwright's shop, still called "The Pigeon Loft" fifty years later, when I came upon one of their nests, years after the pigeons had all gone. At grandfather's I knew where to find the peas for them— in a little sack on a trestle just within the pantry window; but it is not clear in my memory that I was able to whistle to call the pigeons down.

The tiny brick court, sloping up to a door over a step into the wheelwright's yard, had on the right-hand side of it a little "wood-house," tiled, and built of tarred weather boards.

Separating this wood-house from the dwelling-house was a most exciting open channel, all brick-work, which it was a delight, albeit some trouble, to flush with water from the wash-house sink. You see, the wash-house stood opposite to the wood-house, just across the little red brick court where the pigeons hobbled and nodded. The doorway into the wash-house was just past the kitchen window; and under this doorway (I learnt afterwards) was a well, ten feet or so deep. (Similar wells were fairly plentiful along East Street.) Red paving-bricks covered the well, and it fed a pump, immediately within the wash-house door. Under this pump was a stone sink, with outlet into the above-mentioned channel.

But note the cunning tidiness of our forefathers! The waste from the sink was hidden under the paving bricks until it had crossed the little courtyard, but then, against the wood-house, it was allowed to go uncovered.

At the wheelwrights' already I knew about the water-butts standing in that yard to catch rain water for use in "shoeing" wheels. I had watched my father, who had bought a syringe for the purpose, syringing the boarded outbuildings in hot weather, lest the fires for tyring wheels should set light to the buildings. And in the stagnant water-butts the little wriggling red "hammer heads" that were to turn into gnats were a well-known joy.

CHAPTER VII

HOPS

ON the north side of Farnham Street, where now are building estates, with avenues and curbed footpaths and so on, there was in my childhood one long succession—two miles or so, from Coxbridge in the west to Bells Bottom and Hale Church in the east—of hop grounds. ("*Grounds,*" notice. We thought it the mark of a contemptibly ignorant stranger to talk of Hop-gardens.) Several of these grounds had notable names—The Hart Ground for instance. Others were familiar to us with purely local names—Waterman's, Beaver's, Ford's. At what early age I first heard of White-bines and Green-bines, and Kentish Goldens (or Goldings, perhaps) I do not know; or how soon it seemed important to note the degrees of fertility indicated by the different length of poles—eighteen foots, twelve foots, ten foots. I knew, early, that newly planted hops needed only short slender sticks, usually "spile"—or tops of spoiled poles fit only for firing. It was not every year that parsimonious growers would afford new poles; yet every autumn they probably suffered grievously when old poles, too brittle to bear the weight of clusters of hops all but ripe, snapped before some untimely gale and let their precious burden draggle into the muddy soil, or whip to and fro in the wet wind. If this last happened—if the very bine got broken so that its crop withered into brown flimsy bunches called "fliers"—it might be a serious loss, for a pole might easily carry ten or twenty shillings' worth of hops. So, several times I went with my father through his little ground, to see what havoc last night's wind had wrought, and to look on respectfully while he did what repairs he could with string. My little boots would grow heavy with sticky mud at such times.

Of the actual cultivation of hops I knew very little. Always some digging was going on: hop-ground work, I learnt afterwards, employed many an able labourer all the year round; and it was a disgrace to a grower to have weeds in his hop-ground. When a man had dug his "task," he began again. The day was yet far off before any more permanent structure replaced poles for the hops to climb on. Poles had to be put up every spring—three, or else four to a "hill"; and very early (as soon as the growth had fairly started) women went out "tying." The women carried little low stools, and, regardless of weather, sat down patiently to tie every uprising shoot to its pole, so that it might get a good start. Raffia had not been discovered perhaps, or more likely was beyond the women's means. Every tyer brought her own rushes for the purpose; which had been trodden into lissomeness on the cottage floor—as I discovered years afterwards in Bettesworth's cottage, when old Lucy Bettesworth was planning to go out "tying" by and by. It was usually judged that the hops were growing fast enough, if they were "half-way up the poles by midsummer."

Then began anxieties in Farnham. Were the hops coming into bloom properly? Were they at all "lousy"? Was there any sign of "blight," or "mould," or "mildew," or "red-spider"? Were the nights warm enough? Was

71

there too much wind? Towards September old ram-shackle carts full of "gypsies" with sunburnt and un-kempt children, and old sacks, and all sorts of odds and ends—dogs, cats, fowls—came making their leisurely way along the ancient street to this or that hop-ground, days before the picking was due to begin; and those were the days when there might be theft and when timid town dwellers were a little afraid of "tramps" in country places, when as yet the "hoppers" had not begun earning and had time to risk "spoiling their hopping" by some mischief or other. This word "hopping" should be noted, by the way. We never spoke of hop-picking.

Hopping was the season for school-holidays in Farn-ham: a season of blowsy careless open-air life—not too comfortable, yet always enjoyable, with just a touch of excitement in it. It was shabby, jolly; it gave you an appetite. You wore old clothes and might go dirty; and on the whole it was golden and warm September weather—easy-going sunburnt autumn weather. To be sure, "Hop-ping mornings" was a phrase with especial meaning in Farnham: it seemed to fit exactly the early hours, just after sunrise in September, while the air was chilly from the night and fingers ached, and a touch of frost made you wish for breakfast and something hot to drink. The really bad weather for hopping was steady rain, when pickers stayed away altogether, though hundreds would generally draggle into the hop-ground of a morning—say at about half-past six—in hopes that the weather would clear soon. As a rule however I remember hopping as a quiet and glowing time, warm, a little fatigued. September could

even be too fine—too hot. In this case pickers would sometimes make a screen for themselves of poles already
"picked," to shade their "standings" from too wearisome
a spell of sunshine, when you stood hour after hour, picking hops into a basket.

And, even with that screen, hot sun could be really
harmful. A properly ripe hop[1], fit to pick, was firm and
stiff between the fingers and heavy with yellow-golden
dust—and helped to fill the basket: but in hot weather the
hops were limp—"wilty" as we said—and did not soon
enough make up a bushel.

And it was by the bushel that the picking of hops was
paid for. Pickers who were out to earn money—and many
Farnham folk took their annual holiday that way—would
"take a frame," that is to say engage themselves to an
owner of hops, to be responsible for picking into one of his
seven-bushel baskets until the crop was harvested. Up
the insides of the big long baskets black marks measured
the bushels; and if the hops were "wilty" it took too long
to reach and pass one of these marks, and the pickers felt
tired and stifled and cross. At such times a little boy could
get plenty of testy words and sour looks by blundering
carelessly against a basket. The contents would too easily
shake down to show a smaller measure. When the basket
was full enough—at least you hoped it might be full
enough,—you could make it look a little fuller still by
plunging both arms in deep and "lightening" the hops in

---

[1] Such a hop, squarish in shape, and yellowish-green in colour, might be
an inch and a half or two inches long. If, as sometimes happened, little
leaflets grew out of it, it was called a "King Hop."

it. Then you called out "Tallyman"—and the grower's
representative came with his book (no longer tallies, in my
time) to enter what you had picked. He was likely to
scrutinise the basketful rather carefully, lest there should
be too many leaves in it. A certain sort of pickers, out to
make money and working too fast, probably needed looking after. "Scratchers" they were called by other pickers.
The full basket was emptied into a "sarplice"—a wide
open bag of coarse brown sacking, skewered over a wooden
'frame" and hung conveniently near to a "setting" of
pickers. The sarplice (sarplier was its more correct name—
but we lived near Farnham Castle, and may have thought
"sarplice" would sound better to the Bishop) would hold
eighteen bushels or so and then could be skewered up and
swung into a cart and taken to the kiln for drying.

It was a pleasant thing in the dusky autumn evenings to
pass close in Farnham streets to a load of freshly picked
hops. There were many such loads, and most fragrant they
were! The very streets smelt of hops as the cart went
lumbering along and every load of bulging sarplices told
to a native of the town what had been going on all round
him. Truly to think now of the loaded waggons and carts
is to recover weeks of strong rough open-air autumn. Those
plump earth-coloured, yet greenish, sacks, lying a-tumble
all across the cart, meant so much. To see them was to see,
and smell, the picturesque dismantling of a hop-ground—
to hear the day-long chatter as of a flock of depredating
birds; to catch the frequent laugh, the garrulous squabble,
the rustle of the bines, the squalling of children. "Tallyman" has been mentioned; oftener still sounded the cry

74

"Pole-puller"—for every ground had one or two men (I remember one went by the name of "Ginger") whose duty was to keep the pickers supplied with "poles," while of course he was responsible to the grower for due care of the plant. With a strong pocket-knife he cut all the bines of a pole twelve inches or so above the soil; with an ingenious implement called a Hop-dog he lifted the leaf-covered poles up out of the ground; and so he laid them down beside the "frame" they had been allotted to, ready for the pickers to pick up and place over the basket for themselves, as soon as they were ready to gather the crop. (By the way, though the hops grew in bunches, and often a big bunch was torn whole from the bine, the hops had to be separated from it and put into the basket one by one.) I do not remember pole-pullers as individual men; but a memory of showy colour comes to me, soon resolved into sun-tanned skin, hairs shining curly on strong arms, hop-growth and sky; and, on the ground, a pile of men's things—white "slops," yellow straw baskets, a black leather strap or so, a glass bottle with tea showing through it, a dark brown wooden beer-bottle shaped like a tiny barrel. Corduroy trousers and red cotton handkerchiefs add to the gaudy colour effect.

All day long the picking goes on; women scold at their children, who will neither work nor be still. "Let me catch you, you young ninter, I'll gie you the bine!" (the bine being hop bine, tough and twisty, like thin rope—a handy whip). So, for hours, the pickers stand—scolding, laughing, chattering, calling; until at last, between five and six o'clock, the cry goes across the ground "No more poles!"

For in fact enough hops have now been got to keep the kiln going until morning. So, as the poles already "pulled" are finished, the tallyman makes his last round for the day, the sarplices are skewered up and carried to the cart (this is the pole-puller's job, horses being in fact too heavy to travel promiscuously over soil that must always be kept light) and meanwhile the fagged pickers gather together their things and straggle away in little groups or in families.

A spectacle in itself for an hour or two in the autumn evening—from before sunset until dark—was this piece-meal home-going of the Farnham "hoppers." Not that they went, all of them, home every night. There were many gangs of "out-pickers"—families from far away villages, or from the slums of Reading or of West London; and these came to stay until the hopping was over. Certainly it was one of the sights of the town to see some waggon-load of village folk arriving; or weeks later, to see the families going off again in their waggons, close packed; to see, to hear them; for especially on the return journey (glad to be sitting down again and going home) the villagers wedged into their waggons would be singing all along the streets—probably having money in their pockets, or wearing new clothes, or new boots bought in Farnham town. The slum dwellers too had no home to go to. They had but "barricks"—mere shelters with absolutely no sanitary conveniences; while many "gyppoes"—many of "the royal family"—had pitched their tents in the same hop-grounds where they worked all day. But besides all

76

these there were hundreds from the villages near Farnham
—fathers, mothers, children, and all—hundreds who had
locked up their cottages and trudged in out of the country
for the day's work, wet or fine; who every nightfall trudged
back again their mile or two, tired, dirty, hungry.

I was not aware, then, that anybody saw anything
sorrowful in these endless streams of shabby-looking
people along all the country lanes at nightfall—the women
pushing perambulators, the children too often squalling,
many a boy or girl dragging a piece of "spile"—a broken
hop-pole—perhaps for cooking a supper. But after many
years I did hear men like Bettesworth (as I never at any
time heard their "betters") speak compassionately of the
women's weary days. Truly it must have been weary work
for many a cottage woman (though I have no doubt many
husbands helped), seeing that in the cottages, reached at
last, the beds wanted making, while there was some washing up to be done, no water without going to the well, no
tap, no fire or gas. But these things I did not know; and
I never thought of the hoppers' home-going as anything
but jolly. After a day amongst hops, and out of doors, they
were sure to sleep well; and they would not only be hungry;
they would have plenty of relishing food. There was no
doubt about that. If a "hopping morning" was one sign
of the season, so, no less surely, was the smell every night
of herrings frying! "Red herrings" ("Sojers") were the
meal everywhere. Every street or lane rejoiced in the crisp
appetising smell of their cooking. The night air was
fragrant with it.

Another scent, that hung about the whole neighbour-

hood (obviously coming from a bluish vapour that poured
thick from the kilns now and then)—a strong suffocating
smell, came from the brimstone burnt with the drying
hops. Though it made folk cough and was choking to
asthmatic wind-pipes, all Farnham stoutly held that this
brimstone burning was good for the town; fumigating it
wholesomely with sulphur fumes when all those dirty out-
pickers might be bringing in fearful infections from their
slums. While I could still stand this smell (in after years
I could not enter a kiln where hops were drying—it set
me wheezing at once) I liked to see the golden drops that
rained down from brimstone thrown on to the charcoal
fire; better still I liked the potatoes which could be baked
(in their jackets of course) in the ashes under the glowing
grates. The only necessary ingredient was salt, which you
took with you screwed up in a bit of newspaper. Plates and
knives and forks were not needed, no one ever missed them.

The pay for picking was from three-halfpence to four
pence a bushel, according as the crop hung thick on the
poles or needed finding, one hop at a time, under the
leaves. A tedious job it always seemed to me: I never, at
one sitting, exceeded a third of a bushel. In picking, the
golden pollen from the hop flowers made one's fingers
slightly sticky; while the juice stained them black; and
(you found it when you went to wash) the leaves stung the
skin. In the usual absence of pumice-stone I found the
rough stone edge of the sink would rub off the worst of
the stain; but nothing prevented my hands from smarting
—no mottled soap or anything—when I dipped them into
the cold water in the hand-bowl. While picking one would

sometimes find amongst the hops a "lion"—the larva of a lady-bird—and this lion was viewed with favour, as the alleged devourer of "green fly." Once or twice also I found amongst the leaves a "hop-dog[1]"—the huge green caterpillar of, I am told, the hawk moth.

Not only was the picking poorly paid; quite often the picker worked for a day or so actually without knowing what the rate of pay was to be! What could helpless women and children do otherwise than take the best they could get? Only, sometimes a grower over-reached himself; for after all, his crop could not wait for ever, and he ran serious risk, if he failed to make people willing to gather it for him. And they knew it. So my memory holds a dim picture of a "strike"—an old dingy and mean street, a grey morning, and a little gang of people, shabby and with no order, straggling along the street, on their way to the house or shop of the stingy grower. I think they carried tin cans and other instruments of "rough-music." I think too they took for emblems of discontent a black flag, and a penny loaf on the top of a hop-pole, and a red-herring or "sojer." Yet this sort of thing after all was an exception. In another memory I see twilight falling on the long street of Farnham, where (in these old days) there is no wheel traffic unless, now and then, a load of "sarplices" is being carried to a kiln; and the street is thronged—it is Saturday evening—with hoppers loafing from shop to shop, from public-house to public-house. They are sauntering, good-tempered, careless, shabby; one threads in and out through a street full of them.

[1] The pole-puller's tool for levering up hop-poles was also a "hop-dog."

In yet another memory I am, myself, in my grand-father's kitchen (by dim candle-light) while somebody bustles in and out of the pantry to draw beer and carry it into the adjoining sitting-room. For there my grandfather is "paying-off" hoppers. The old man (I must have peeped in at him) is at his usual table, looking very alert and capable; and perhaps he needed to be severe, for in the kitchen, beside the tallow candle, my aunt (or my elder sister perhaps) speaks of some "dreadful" man there—who may be seen, in another peep, to stand black-avised, scratching, furtive, unwashed, opposite my grandfather. But all is well where my grandfather is.

When the picking was over the hop-growers had by no means done. First they had to market their crop; and then to start again, getting their hop-ground cleared up and ready for another year.

The marketing of course was preceded by drying and bagging. The hop-dryer had special tools, notably a very large but light wooden spade for shifting the hops on the "hair-cloth" in the kiln, on which they were spread over the fires to dry and take the required tint and smell from the brimstone fumes. When dried they were heaped up at the end of the kiln, to be ready for bagging.

This was on an upper floor. For the "bag" (a very stiff and thick canvas, yet not too strong for so precious a load) was hung down through a hole in the floor, so that the hops could be easily shovelled into it. An "engine" fixed above it to the woodwork of the kiln enabled the dryer to screw the hops down, until the "pocket" of them was full. (From underneath the hop-pocket showed as a pale cylinder, tight and hard, reaching up through the ceiling.) A full pocket of hops had to be carefully weighed—scales for this purpose being kept in every kiln. It usually weighed about two and a half hundred-weight.

Once, perhaps oftener, I watched my father "drawing a sample" from a pocket of hops—a job to fill any Farnham man with pride, and performed in a sort of religious silence. With what reverence one seam of the pocket was ripped open far enough for the sample-drawers (a special implement of shining steel blades and screws) to be properly thrust in! Imagine two or three grave men at this job, anxious, holding their breath. At last the sample is carefully lifted out—a solid brick of dried hops some three inches square by six or seven inches long—and is passed from hand to hand for criticism. Did it consist of hops not crumbled into dust? Was there a good proportion of golden pollen in it? Was it a bright green colour, without too many brown patches—a sign of belated picking? All being well the sample might mean a fortune for the anxious grower. Well or ill, it was carefully wrapped up in the best brown paper that money could buy—shiny brown paper, very stiff and tough; and this parcel (proudly carried under the arm) was wound round and round in great lengths of strong string. It was never tied up, for whenever you met another hop-grower it had to be solemnly submitted to his inspection.

Perhaps the string was more firmly knotted when the owner of the sample at last took it with him to Weyhill Fair. But of this I knew nothing; I did not even know that many growers were accompanied to the Fair by their

wives, and that the visit was a sort of annual holiday.
I dimly remember waking one October morning dawn,
and seeing my father in the cold-looking dusk starting to
catch a train for Weyhill. He came back at night, presumably well pleased, for he had toys for us children. But
he never had much to do with hops, and certainly never
made his fortune by his little dabblings in that gamble.
I think he was always at the mercy of growers on a larger
scale, who picked and dried for him when it suited their
convenience.

After the hopping it was woman's work, paid by the
piece, to strip the poles where they lay in heaps just as the
pickers had left them. The bines tossed together into brown
heaps were carted away and stacked in ricks, for litter—
especially for pigs.

The poles (the spile having been sorted out from them)
were piled up into "aisles," and looked like tents all across
the hop-ground. There they stood throughout the winter,
restoring to the ground a look of order. It was needed.
For indeed all was untidy and desolate when first the hops
were down. It seemed as if winter had come; and it was
a common remark that the cold had been let in upon Farnham town. Certainly the wide hop-ground everywhere
looked bleak and desolate. The soil had been trodden flat
by the pickers; here and there a solitary pole, left standing
for some reason, stood gaunt and naked to the weather.
Occasionally a rook would settle atop of the pole; or
occasionally a battered tin can would be put there. Yet the
untidy hop-grounds made a fine playground for boys; one
felt it a proud thing, too, to climb one of the hop-poles.

Soon, in the winter, a new set of smells began, cheerfully endured, if not indeed approved, in the town. For the sake of the hops we felt it right that the whole neighbourhood should reek of trotters, of guano, or any nameless filth the growers chose for manure.

Another thing too marked the winter. New poles, to replace the spile, were carted into the hop-ground, and had to be pointed there. I suppose this was for the hop-ground man to do. With one hand the man held the pole down on a block a little lower than his knee, with the other hand he swung down on the pole a light axe. And the axe must have been sharp, and the hand that swung it strong, for five or six chops pointed the pole. I was too little to know or care much about this work, though I liked very well to see a man at it, so deft, so industrious. With his trousers strapped or tied under the knees, and with a short pipe in his mouth, the man almost always looked good-tempered. Why not? It was probably not too well paid a job—piecework, and with the chips for a perquisite; but it was out-o'-doors; and with every blow of the axe a gratified sensation would run up the man's arm—the sensation of a touch from the outside world that is not one's-self.

CHAPTER VIII

THE MEADOWS

The Churchyard had not yet been levelled. Not yet, as now, could its turf be clipped like a lawn. It was thick with graves—many of them rounded up in uncompromising red-brick grown dark with age; and here and there was a big built-up "vault" with iron railing round it. The presence of the dead was allowed to look grim; yet you could scamper over the lower graves, if you liked, leaping from one to the other; and on the lush grass between them many sheep browsed.

The Churchyard was crossed by various public footpaths and could therefore never be shut for the night. For the same reason the iron gate (if indeed there was a gate) in the south-west corner of the wall stood always unfastened. An oak turnstile served further to keep back cattle and sheep at the narrow pathway to "The Meadows" there. The meadows were known as "The Church Meadows." Just beyond them stretched—far and wide, and very peaceful to see on summer evenings—"The Bishop's Meadows." The Bishop of Winchester, as Lord of the Manor, was a very important man in Farnham in those days; and he probably had considerable interest in The Bishop's Meadows. Be that as it may, they lay widespread and full of light—a pastoral setting to the snug tiled town, right away from the Church Meadows to Wrecclesham a mile off. At due seasons hay-making was going on in the meadows; at other times there were

84

bullocks there or browsing sheep, very peaceful; and always, all the year round, those pastures—looking so boundless from a child's three-foot height—were crossed by lines, stretching into far distance, of ancient withies along the various watercourses. (I prefer the local word: "willows" always seemed finicking.) On hot summer evenings you would see cattle standing in the river, meditatively flicking their tails.

Not only did the gentle "Wey" itself traverse these silent spaces; channels from it were cut here and there, for flooding the meadows, or for controlling the supply to various water-mills which still served Farnham people. Thus, if you crossed from the Churchyard to Weydon Mill, in that five or ten minutes there were three little bridges to pass over—the first of them was over a mere ditch, the last of them over another ditch close under the paling of Weydon Mill garden. These two bridges were but guarded by wooden stiles—one stile so low that you could easily step over it, the other involving only an easy clamber. There you came to the mill and a road over the river itself. There you left the meadows and the little water ruts. A shallow ford beside the last stile, a ford readily barred by a pole, admitted cattle into the meadows—the cattle had stabbled the ground at the ford into mud here and there— or perhaps gave access to hay waggons. This stile and the other one left behind at the Church Meadows sufficed to keep the animals turned out to graze from straying beyond their bounds; so there was no need for a stile at all across the intervening bridge, though a pole was sometimes slung across it—if the Bishop's Meadows were "laid-up for grass," or if the actual hay-making was going on; but as a rule this middle bridge was wholly open. A rather singular bridge, now I think of it. As it was meant for hay waggons to cross the stream, so it was almost level in itself and not raised above the path at either end. Stout narrow planks were what it was built of—an easy continuation across the stream of the pathway—a safe and smoothish grey floor. I ought to know. For often I have lain down there on my belly, to gaze down into the slow water. The next little bridge—well, I lay on that too if I wanted to; shoals of tiny fish might be watched there— little hurrying streaks of blackness—or groups of miraculous summer "skaters" walking on the water, or a score or so of waggling tadpoles. Yet all these were three feet or so below one, the gravel was not so comfortable to sprawl on, and one had to scramble up if anybody else wanted to pass over. But at the bridge half way across the meadows there was plenty of room. There, on the planks, one could lie at peace, kicking up heels into the spacious meadowland air, careless of passers-by and oblivious of all but the placid stream scarce eighteen inches below one's face. A pleasant moist weedy smell was wafted up from it; for thick tresses of water weed, combed by the water, softly swayed and rippled along the length of the stream-bed. And in the magic spaces between the long dark clumps of weeds, now and then a small fish crossed mysteriously, may-be some "miller's thumb" or other. Very pleasant it was to see a miller's thumb come from nowhere and tuck his head under a stone at the bottom of the water. As he stayed there—foolishly thinking himself hidden,

86

I supposed—he waved his tail in the water. It was too tempting. I put my hand in to take him; and then suddenly he was gone. Why not? I didn't want him; an idle cat could have withstood the temptation as easily; but I didn't really want the miller's thumb. I merely liked well to be there, not knowing that life could ever be less peaceful. There was so much room in those meadows. A comfort too was without doubt added—though I neither realised it then nor wished for more—by knowing that it was possible to vary one's route further afield. Across the grass a footpath—cracked in summer, awfully, by earthquakes, we used to say—twisted in and out towards Passmore Bridge at Wrecclesham. For a time the path kept close to the river; one could fish as one went home, with a bent pin on cotton trailed in the water; and at one spot the path led by a solitary withy. In very early years I travelled this way with my elder sister, and the meadows were enhanced by my knowing of that footpath; yet soon I left off going there and at last forgot all about it. Perhaps long grass hid it from childish eyes; perhaps hay-making once spoilt the comfort of it—for hay-makers could bawl or swear alarmingly if one got in the way. Anyhow I left off straying by that path; yet a vague memory of it winding away westwards may have improved the meadows for me, as I lay on the familiar bridge, watching the fish and smelling the weedy smell.

If you chose to get out of the meadows altogether you might still keep them in view from The Hatches. In later years I found that a pleasant walk under the sloping river bank, with young firwoods (for hop-poles) planted there. Close by—you must mind not to fall in—the slow river brimmed its banks against its own meadows on the other side, and here it was good to see patches of yellow water-lilies, or flies dancing in and out amongst the rushes. But as a little child I rarely got so far from home as The Hatches. Oftener I went to another set of meadows—The Bush Meadows, away to the East. The gas works overlooked them; but I never saw so far as all that—more than a quarter of a mile away. To my three-foot-high sight, the Bush Meadows were boundless. As one crossed towards the Penstock and another mill—Hatch Mill—the footpath took one past two or three ancient-looking posts which I now believe to have marked "Lammas Lands." The grass didn't grow long, though it was very green, round about those posts. Cattle, rubbing against them, had trodden a slight hollow round each one; and these spots looked even a little desolate, when all the rest of the meadow was asway with flowering "grass" laid up for the hay. What fun to wade through the grass! Yet one did not wade, for that would have been wrong—or at least one did not wade much.

Only, at a certain time of the year there were flowers one so badly wanted in that growing grass, not to be got elsewhere. I daresay there were other sorts, but I remember only "milkmaids" ("Our Lady's Smocks," or "smell-smocks") and "broad buttercups" ("Marsh marigolds"). Even to a man five feet up the May meadows are sunny with buttercups spread out in sheets, but to a little child down in the very glory itself the flower-growth was wide and lavish rapture. Why we picked these flowers plentifully, clutching them into our little hot hands and, likely enough, carelessly throwing them away after all—this shall be told by and by, but I will finish with the meadows first.

Just before we came to the mill, with its loud foaming rush of water from the Penstock, there was a nice wooden bridge to cross. Clattering over the boards one felt so safe there, between the railings on both sides—wooden railings, green from long years of weather, and smooth to the touch and the sight. If you didn't cross to the mill, you might wander in and out by the river; but this I did not do for years. And in fact all that part of the meadows seemed forbidden ground, and somehow had no mystery or spaciousness to tempt one to explore. It may have been near there that "Brown's Hole" was, where my father had learnt to swim in his boyhood; but that had no interest for a little timid child, too liable to catch cold and terribly afraid of it. Only, I knew what other boys meant in the summer, when I overheard them talk of "going down to get in." They meant going down to the river, probably to Brown's Hole. Another phrase was sometimes overheard; when some angry boy or other invited another angry boy to "come on down the medders!" That was a challenge to fight in some lonelier place; and I always thought, though without certain knowledge, that the chosen site was the Church Meadows, if not the more spacious Bishop's Meadows, where a fight was less likely to be interrupted.

CHAPTER IX

COMMEMORATIONS

REAL buttercups—those brilliant and very shiny flowers, whose conspicuous yellow lights up the sunny roadsides in May when the glory of dandelions is getting over—real buttercups have this value for little children: they can be used to prove that a child likes butter. The way is to hold the flower close up to the child's chin, so that the yellow reflection from it may shine on the delicate skin. Incidentally, the chin looks very pretty—as I lately saw when two youngsters in the road were putting this very matter to the test; but of course the main thing is to discover if you really like butter. In my own case I never heard that there was any doubt at all on that point. The proof was as convincing as the test whether or no you could eat any more. If the skin across your forehead was loose enough to be pushed sideways under the finger-tips—not your own finger-tips, but a fond aunt's or grandmother's—plainly there was still room for more stuffing within. But this was not such a happy and dimpling proof as the proof that you liked butter.

"Broad buttercups," whether good for this or not, had special values of their own, besides that they could be gathered plentifully into big nosegays and lasted well in a basin of water, bringing juicy spring and sunshine into the sitting-room. For one thing the rich flowers and leaves, mingled with pale mauve "milkmaids," could be used in the following way: between two pieces of glass (the squarer the better) you pressed a little arrangement of flowers. Then round the double thickness of glass you folded brown paper. Fastened on one side of the glass—perhaps gummed—the paper formed a background for the flowers within; left loose, in a flap, on the other side, it could be opened like the cover of a book to show the buttercups and milkmaids flattened between the two pieces of glass, and then you said "A pin to see the peepshow." Whether you ever got even so much as a pin I do not know. Undoubtedly tokens of affection were got; for my memories of that little childish display seem delicious as the colours and the fresh juiciness of the crushed flowers.

But the chief value, after all, of broad-buttercups and milkmaids was for making garlands for May Day. Not that any of us Sturts ever carried garlands. That was a sign of poverty; for on May Morning (a school holiday) little troops and families of cottage children, gay as the spring, carried round to all houses their posies tied to sticks, their careful wreaths and crosses made of milkmaids and buttercups, probably mingled with daisies and wall-flowers and may-be blue-bells; and the children collected half-pennies, singing their ditty:

"The first of May is Garland Day,
So please remember the Garlands."

On that same morning the chimney-sweeps came round, gathering largess. A wonder it was to see that their oddly familiar faces, usually sooty, were really much the same colour as other people's. Their voices proved who they were, as they sang and danced, clattering their hand-brushes against their wooden shovels and one of them "playing the bones" held between his knuckles. What they sang I do not in the least remember; it was probably some appeal for coppers, appropriate to the day, and was meant to be festive. In fact, my memory of the lads dancing is a little sad. They had come through from the street to our back yard—two or perhaps three half-grown lads, already crooked from overwork; and there in the forenoon sunlight they danced and clattered and sang. Yet though they were bedecked with ribbons and laughed and made merry, the merriment was rather obviously "made." Perhaps the contrast with their usual sootiness was too great; perhaps they were too plainly conscious of having but this one day's holiday in the year, and of being obliged to use it for foolishness and for appealing for alms. At any rate their polished faces, grinning for the customary laugh, have left in me a memory, for more than half a century, of forlornness. It is none of the prattling gaiety that clings still to my other May fancies of the children having a holiday, trooping round with their garlands, and singing their old-world ditty to the old-world tune.

Of other commemorations of the seasons I don't remember much. "Shik-shak" is a word I seem to have known all my life; yet I was a biggish schoolboy before the importance of keeping "Shik-shak Day" (Oak-apple Day) came home to me. Then I knew that you were beneath contempt, as well as in danger of being pinched or kicked, if you could not "show your shik-shak." It was not necessary, though it may have been splendid, to flaunt an actual oak-apple in your cap. The very secrecy of this celebration may have recommended something different; and it was quite common (I don't know why, but the thing was worth doing) to delude another boy into thinking he had a victim in you. Then, at the very moment when he was about to kick you indignantly, you pulled out, from some hidden place—your boot perhaps—a bit of oak-leaf that, however bruised, proved you a true believer after all. Strangely, no-one ever got angry about this— it was a joke; but I do remember dimly an angry time when somebody's crumpled oak-leaf was suspected of being maple.

Other anniversaries I recognised (not to speak of Christmas, described in another book) were Valentine's Day, and April Fool's Day. Both of these are associated in my memory with the little shop. In the shop itself a stock of valentines had to be provided for the 14th of February. My mother never let herself down to the level of selling "ugly" valentines—loathsome things meant to be offensive—but she willingly stocked and sold any kind of sentimental "effusion." Every Valentine's Eve there was sure to steal into the shop some shy country chap or other to spend his hard-earned pence on some soft-hearted declaration of love for a sweetheart. In the course of years these things became so costly (there were frilly-edged scented valentines in shiny pasteboard boxes, up to half-a-crown apiece) that the trade was too expensive and had to be abandoned. Cheaper Christmas cards did something to kill it. But in my childhood everybody regarded St Valentine's Day. Some mystery about the first person (of the other sex) you chanced to see on that fateful morning

93

never got really home to my infantile understanding—but to make our own valentines—when was I not big enough for that? At the round table in the little back attic we engaged busily in this manufacture. With scissors and a cunning yet easy device we cut and folded make-shift frilly rims, and with gum or starch we stuck them on to our note-paper, already embellished with a drawing. In later years I liked to do a Christmas Card with holly and a robin—for both of which the red crayon came in handy. But in the palmy days of valentines my sister was the artist. Very pointed, not to say sharp, were the noses of the ladies she drew, very full of feathers were their hats, very ornate with scalloped edges were their ample skirts. If they needed crimped hair we were always willing to oblige when asked to "Shake please!" because you could do crimped hair better if the table shook. It was odd— but we hardly noticed it then—that the feet of these ladies were central under their skirts and had no relation at all to their bodies. "The chalks" came in for colouring: yellow (substitute for golden) for hair, green or pink for dresses, and so on. These chalks, pointed and no bigger than half a slate pencil, were obtained about ten at a time, in little card-board cases covered with starry paper, and soon disappeared. But they were better regarded than the commoner slate pencil—generally an inch or so long and too short to be pointed, but sometimes (kept in a shallow wooden pencil-case) covered with paper and sharpened quite to a point. What child now knows how to sharpen a slate pencil—holding it down on a school desk for steadier knife work, or grinding it to an acute but ill-shaped angle on the wall or a stone or a sink edge or a street kerb? What child knows the hideous shriek of a pencil held vertical on a slate, only too likely to set your teeth on edge? Or what child knows about a slate itself—grey when new, dark when old and greasy; or how to clean it without a sponge by breathing—never say spitting—on it? Or why ink is recommended for it? or how it should be framed, or what it feels like when it is cracked all across? or how to play "Up to London" on a slate? But no such matters made valentines too familiar to us, or cheapened the idea of the chalks that one coloured them with.

All Fools' Day is associated in my mind with a memory I have long hesitated to record, I am so ashamed of it—when I made an April Fool of my mother herself, and thought it clever. But indeed I had no idea then that she might be weary; it was years afterwards before she became hopelessly crippled as a result of overwork—running up and down stairs, wringing-out blankets from the wash-tub, and so on for twelve hours a day or more. I wantonly added to her burden that First of April. Breakfast was over; she, with no minutes to waste, was making beds in the attic while downstairs we were expecting every minute the parcel of newspapers to arrive from the railway station; for it must have been half-past seven o'clock. Heaven knows what time my mother had got up. We had been washed and dressed, breakfast was done; perhaps my father, home from his wheelwright's shop, was taking down the newspaper shop shutters, or perhaps he was away in the back loft watering his flowers. At any rate my mother, at top of the house, seemed fair game. And I remembered the date! Can it not be guessed what I did? I was on the look-out for "the truck" from the Station; and since it did not come and I was wanting something to do, I trotted to the foot of the stairs and called "Papers!" It was the usual signal. Down came my mother at a run; to find that her urgent task could not yet begin; and that I was calling her an April Fool! Certainly I was not spanked; nor was I, to the best of my belief, even scolded. I may even have boasted that I had made an April Fool without actually telling a lie.

Of course all the family birthdays were celebrated, besides the birthdays of various uncles and aunts and cousins. I watched too for "Pancake Day" on Shrove Tuesday, for Hot Cross Buns on Good Friday. I knew the First Sunday in Advent was called "Stir up Sunday," the collect for the day at church beginning with the words "Stir up." Not a few Farnham folk recognised the opening of Weyhill Hop Fair on the 13th October by choosing to regard that as the first day when you might have a fire to sit by, but we were not so unhappy as that.

But I have omitted one odd thing. Why was All Fools' Day supposed to be over by noon? If you were so misguided as to trick anybody after that hour, you might be told

"April Fool day's gone and past,
So you're the greatest fool at last!"

FARM LABOURER,
SURREY

COTTAGE INTERIOR, c. 1860

HOP PICKING

HOP GARDEN

SHARPENING
WITH
BAGGING
HOOKS

THE WOODCUTTER

PLUCKING GEESE

FARRIER

CHAPTER X

"PAPER-BOYS"

WHEN not in use the "truck" mentioned in the previous chapter stood in the yard at the Wheelwright's Shop; where it had been built, if not by my father himself, certainly to his orders. A little light hand-cart it was— a panelled box (made for strength) with **T** handle; all lead-coloured, running on red hand-made wheels, it being long before the day of imported "Warner" wheels. The truck, being only an open box, served for bringing us chips and blocks from the wheelwright's; but its main use was for the morning papers. Two boys took it to the station, threw into it the parcel of newspapers, then brought it at a run to the shop, to outpace other news-agents' boys. You could hear divers trucks rattling along the ancient street, little other traffic being about at half-past seven.

The bundle of newspapers, wrapped in rough brown paper and old news-bills, was hurriedly thrown out on to the shop floor, where the string was cut as quickly as could be. There was no such thing as untying knots, or even looking to cut near a knot, for string was plentiful, customers were impatient (one or two would be already waiting, getting in the way) and there was much to do. Especially was there much to do in rainy weather. For probably the parcel had been put out from the train on to a wet platform, stabbled with mud; and sometimes the papers came with their margins a mere muddy pulp which had to be trimmed away with scissors; and that made the rest of the work difficult.

For in those days the papers did not come folded singly. They reached us in quires, and the newsagent then had to separate and fold them, and count them too. In later years I took my share in folding papers—thousands and thousands must have passed through my hands. But at the earlier time my mother must have done the bulk of it, though she had her own sister to help her, and my elder sister doubtless did a part. The brunt of the work fell on my mother, who indeed had only the distributing to do besides, and the shop to mind until eight or nine at night, with invoices and bills, and us children and my father to wait on, and cooking and washing and mending and bed-making to see to and a few things like that.

Boys—two or three then—carried out the papers, brought in the money for them, and often used some of it for themselves and had to be dismissed. Not in all cases. I recall six or seven boys who turned out so well that my father was glad at last to draft them into his shop and make wheelwrights of them[1]. In this way I found friends. Often I accompanied the paper-boy on his rounds. Hole was just before my time. Then came George Hammond. One day—we were on the sunny side of Castle Street—some shameless boy across the street called out "Gammon!" It rhymed, near enough, to my companion's name; and being meant as an insult to him had to be

---

[1] Of these Harry Hole was still in the shop 57 years afterwards; and two Keens, two Pharos, and George Hammond must be remembered with appreciation.

checked. Probably Hammond chased the miscreant—
I do not remember. I do remember going into my friend's
home in Bear Lane, to see a model of a farmyard he had
cut out and pasted on to a stout cardboard.

It was George Pharo (already described as a "guy" on
squib night) who wheeled me in the perambulator under
the Bridge at Bridge Square, when "The River" was very
low; and no doubt I owed many other pleasures to that
fearless spirit. But of all the paper-boys who delighted me,
I best liked Bill—but I will not name him—call him Bill
Wriggler.

Bill one summer morning went into a little shop in
West Street and bought some ripe gooseberries, which he
invited me to share. I declined; and presently I noticed
that at every step he scrooped! How glad was I then that
I had not had a gooseberry! But long afterwards (years
perhaps) I was able to trace an exactly similar scroop to
a pair of corduroy trousers! Gooseberries had nothing to
do with it. Bill Wriggler—it may have been later in the
same day—introduced me to the kitchen in his cottage
where I partook of a rasher of bacon. Kitchen? It was
rather the tap-room (empty then, with forms beside a deal
table) of a public house in one of Farnham's back lanes;
yet what a visit! I have never passed that place since without recalling the relishing food, which I think was then
new to me. Well might I remember Bill Wriggler!

And he it was who entranced me with his tales. Like
other paper-boys in my mother's service, after the papers
had been taken out he used to help at cleaning boots, and
scouring knives and forks too, in the shed; and I would sit

by and look and listen. Even to look was interesting enough. The boots were first brushed bare of mud with a hard brush; then the blacking was put on. The blacking was mixed, wherever it came from, in one of the red earthenware dishes in which flower pots are stood; and though the best way to moisten it was to take it to the pump in the wash-house, the easier plan of spitting into it was often preferred. It was then smeared by the grimy "blacking brush" in a thin black paste on the boot you held on your fist; and then came the tiresome job of shining the boot with the "shining brush." A warm job this, which might take too long, if you didn't know how to go to work, or if your fingers, instead of tightening up under the leather, let it go limp against the shining-brush. Bill Wriggler would sometimes let me try. (In later years, my mother having so little time, I would "clean boots" myself on Sunday mornings.)

While at this work, Bill Wriggler could talk; and I listened, fascinated. What other romances he had I do not at all remember now; but there was one I never since found equalled in any book. For Bill told of an uncle of his who owned, think of it! an island. And on this island were groves of trees; and in the trees no cheap everyday sparrows, but, ye gods, canaries! These were the priceless property of Bill's uncle; and I believed every word of it. We, in fact, had a canary ourselves—a captive in a cage; fed on rape, with groundsel and chickweed tucked in between the wires; yellow canvas being pinned round the lower inches of the cage to keep the rubbish from being scratched out too much. In this cage poor "Dicky" lived for a few years; and it never occurred to anybody that he might be dying of loneliness, or even going out of his poor little wits in solitary confinement. At least he looked pretty; twittered pleasantly; and lo! Bill Wriggler's uncle had groves full of such fairy things; in an island too! Of course I loved to listen; and of course I remember the afternoons in the old shed, cool yet full of reflected light and sunshine, worthy of the island of fancy itself.

I remember but little more about the "paper-boys." There was one, his name forgotten, who got into serious trouble because my aunt had heard him call across the street to another boy, "See you damned first," which being told to my mother, was received with horror very salutary to me.

I have a very hazy memory of going once up steep steps to a house, never seen but that once, just beyond Bourne Mill. It must have been one of the paper-boys who took me, but him I do not remember at all. One thing only has kept me from quite losing memory of this unique visit; on a lawn in front of a low-built house, tethered to a tree or trees there, was a monkey—not a very big monkey, but still a monkey for all that, and so unusual a thing that I have never forgotten seeing it.

The nearest thing I ever did myself to delivering papers —it must have been in school holidays—was to fetch occasionally *The Times* from one reader's house and carry it to another. *The Times* being 3*d*. a copy (or perhaps more at that time) was sometimes shared, the first subscriber relinquishing it at noon; and I was man enough to do the exchanging. Three places I seem to have seen on these terms—being "the little boy who had come for, or brought," *The Times*—and I am not sorry now to have penetrated into those parts of old Farnham, which must otherwise have remained unknown to me. In West Street down a dark passage was a side-door, and the passage had on it the name "Drinkwater"—probably the person whose house I had to go to. But there was better than this. Shadowy because of high evergreen hedges on either hand was the backway winding through the shrubbery to Miss Currie's back-door at Fir Grove House. Not shadowy at all was the kitchen door at Captain Mackenzie's in Castle Street. There—I fancy the way to it was at the back and down a basement—were to be seen pale well-scrubbed dresser and kitchen table; and, in a row hanging to a wall, shining dish covers; and how cheerful everything looked!

CHAPTER XI

FAIRS

In my childhood Farnham had three fairs during the year. The first may have been originally a religious occasion, for it was held on Ascension Day, but it was afterwards fixed for May 10th. Midsummer Day was the date for the second; and the third was on the 13th—afterwards changed to the 10th—of November. I don't know whether the incidence of the second on St John's Day had anything to do with the matter, but the Midsummer Fair was commonly called a Pleasure Fair, as if to contrast it against the others, though they all alike seemed to me opportunities for shouting men to drive horses, cattle, and especially sheep. Occasionally some strange wild-looking man would come into the town with sheep—some shepherd not used to streets at all, but only at home on a lonely down, where he never saw or was seen by anybody but his flock and his dog. Perhaps not in those far-off days (though one never knows) but in after years there would fall on me amidst the hubbub and stench of the thronged fair, an influence from the shy wild look of a stranger, as if he had brought with him views of blue horizons and bleak wide skies.

Fair Day was a holiday at all the Farnham schools; farmers wanted to see their sons from the Grammar School or Poppleton's, their daughters from Miss Stratford's; and of course the shop-keepers (by no means "superior" persons or "high-brows" then) had to observe the day. Whether the Fair began overnight I cannot now remember. By the time I was a young man mumpers from all the neighbourhood—having waited in the near lanes for hours, would come hurrying in to the town on the previous evening at the stroke of six (church bell or town-hall clock), and stake out their "standings" in Castle Street. But at any rate in my earliest years the Fair was already in full blast o'mornings when I woke up for the day. Already could be heard unwonted noises from down in the street; and one had not to look long to see down below a hurry of strange sights—a herd of black Welsh bullocks coming over from Blackwater Fair, a dishevelled gang of gypsies, a flock of sheep thronging the street from side to side, sheep dogs rushing and barking to keep slow sheep on the move and in order, a little group of farmers (not, as on market days, in their best clothes), a show cart, a dirty gig or two, unkempt mumpers quarrelling and spoiling for a fight at public-house doors, hard-faced travelling women with sticky-looking brown hair; and at times, as if all this straggling, careless, swearing, jostling crowd were not enough, along the street would come yelling, while the road was just cleared and no more by folk who gave no other heed, a shady-looking fellow—a horse coper—running a frightened horse for sale. No other heed? Not quite so, either. Anybody with a whip, and there were many—gyp, farmer, half-and-half—was liable to crack it loudly, for the fun of frightening the horse into a faster trot. And above the yells, the bleatings, the clatter of horse-hooves, and loud chatter and other name-less noises, came the thin toot of toy trumpets bought at a stall, the cries of showmen, the bang of beetle, driving into the road the stakes for some "cokernut"-shy or still unfinished stall. Guns popped at shooting galleries; children squalled; oh! there wasn't half a din!

Of course one had to hurry out to see the fun; yet the racket in the usually staid street was almost alarming. Fortunately there were hands ("puddies") of rather braver people—a brother, and, bigger still, a sister—to hold on to. Thus fortified one could visit the nearer stalls—first Bonny Rogers's year after year in the Borough, opposite "The Queen's Head." There it was customary to buy gingerbread—thick hunks made for the Fair, or circular disks embellished with lemon peel which had to be removed. Hunks or disks, it was none of it really nice —gingerbread a trifle bitter even—yet the occasion made it palatable. And that was the case when, hurrying to a quiet back street, we added to our gingerbread a supply of "Garibaldi" biscuits. Even then I almost disliked "Garibaldis"—so chucky and tough, looking like baked flies. Yet, as we never bought them at any other time, they were a sign of Fair Day, and I ate them. Round the corner from the Borough three or four more stalls stretched up Castle Street. Big coarse "sugar-sticks," "hundreds and thousands," "hard-bake," could be had at one stall, china dogs and no doubt other shiny crockery-ware things at another.

Beyond came a dingy medley; a swinging-boat or two— already full of louts and squeaking hoydens—and swinging so far across the pavement that you couldn't pass safely without hugging close in to the houses; a popping shooting-gallery; a man supplying a saucer of whelks (vinegar and pepper too, of course) to some pleased looking villager; and in and out, everywhere, a shabby tangle of shabby people not knowing how to be idle, yet bent on doing nothing but be amused for once.

Soon, fifty yards or so farther on, the sheep pens began; and these stretched all up Castle Street on one side and round the corner out of sight—a furlong or so of pens of huddling and bleating sheep. Probably the sheep were frightened; but they could not run away. One could look (not being very tall oneself) into their silly eyes; with a stick (and every boy who was a boy had to have a stick on Fair Day—not a finicking cane or dandified stick either, but a useful thing, ash or nut or withy, cut from a hedge, like a farmer's)—with it one could poke into any sheep's fleece at pleasure, not to learn anything about the animal, but because that was the thing to do. Were not other boys and men at it? All up and down the pavement, and in the roadway beyond the narrow line of sheep, people were wandering—or some were sitting on the hurdles which made the sides of the pens. The people may have been farmers at business, or drovers, or idlers; but it was the thing to tickle your stick into the close South-Down wool, and no sheep could prevent you.

Across the street (I seldom went that side) were first, I think, a few pig pens; but, even before the turn at the upper end of the street was reached, little groups could be seen of scared cows and heifers. These were not penned in; but each group was kept from straying by a man or two with a stick, willing enough to whack back into place any weary or uneasy beast that tried to get away. Round the corner—right away past Castle Steps and even up to "The Grange"—the road for a quarter of a mile was thick with cattle of all sorts. There probably was no great danger there, but I can only remember seeing it once. It was truly no place for a little boy.

Towards dinner-time the Borough and West Street for fifty yards or so, to-day alive with motor-cars, began to fill up with rows of horses. They stood with their tails towards the pavement, facing towards the street they half blocked; and though they stood patient enough, it was not altogether pleasant on the thronged pavement, behind their flicking tails and stamping hooves. Besides, the men who gathered about these horses were a sinister-looking lot, cunning, shifty of eye, loud of speech. I avoided the horses even more timidly than I avoided the cattle. And perhaps there was reason for this too. For it was terrible to see a horse "running," to hear the owner who held the halter keeping up his hullaballoo all through the swaying crowds in the street. It may have been fun to others; it seemed death to me. The horses were often tied together in groups, and not a few of the groups were New Forest Ponies. Harness there was none; but in many cases bright yellow straw had been knotted into tail or mane.

As the day wore on and the cattle and sheep and horses disappeared, Castle Street filled up more and more with "shows" and lounging villagers bent on pleasure. I think the cokernut-shy had not quite ousted the more ancient Aunt Sally; certainly not wooden balls but thick sticks about eighteen inches long were the missiles. They were usually thrown whirling from one end, but one clever man tossed his sticks level from the middle and won too many cokernuts. There was a rich selection of fat ladies, bearded ladies, abortions of all sorts. Some of the shows were fronted with platforms with steps up to them, where mountebanks could address the public—"Walk up! Walk up! Ladies and Gentlemen," or musicians could deafen them with trumpet and drum; and many "shows" were alluring with gaudy paintings on the outside.— Royal Bengal Tigers, Kings, Slaves—I cannot recall what. For I went into none of these shows though I would have liked to go. Not once could any of the seniors with me be persuaded to venture on such a treat.

But two or three minor shows I did get into; and I can still conjure up a recollection of grey-looking damp-looking canvas for their tents. In one of them you did but walk round, putting one eye to a hole, through which a view could be seen. It was a dismal show—as cheerful as squinting into a tiny microscope let into the end of a pen-holder and seeing perhaps Windsor Castle or The Crystal Palace—a wonder we sometimes failed to wonder at. In this gloomy "peep-show" of Farnham Fair might be seen "The Relief of Lucknow," or "The Coronation of Queen Victoria" or some other equally exciting spectacle. There were but nine or ten peep-holes in all; and, I think, but three or four disillusioned patrons solemnly going round besides myself, to hide the spaces of weather-beaten tent; so that one felt very forlorn within and quite glad to come out. But in another tent, where the proprietors appreciated a little better the value of excitement, a crowd

of men and women seated on wooden forms watched per-
forming canaries. The canaries were hauling tiny buckets
up tiny windlasses—doing all sorts of useless and interesting things, the exhibitor of them being a conjuror. Can it
have been the same man, I wonder, in the same dingy
little tent, who worked a certain well-remembered miracle
before my very eyes? I see at any rate, in a certain little
suffocating tent about the colour of slate-pencil, a huddle
of people so close together as to be almost on top of one
another, watching tricks at a table. The people were in
smock frocks—I was wedged in amongst them; and how
the man at the table borrowed a chimney-pot hat from
amongst the audience, and made a pudding in it, has
already been told. My memory of the occasion dies clean
away after the distribution of the pudding. I don't know
what became of the hat. It was probably given back un-
hurt to its owner.

In the late afternoon it became possible to buy little
penny squirts—forerunners of "ladies' tormentors";
though hardly so far off may one date the cry "All the fun
of the fair!" Late in the afternoon too, while the throngs
of people thickened, the roundabouts began to be busy.
I never rode on one. In fact, about tea-time I seem to have
forsaken the Fair and gone home; for no memory remains
of any evening there. Once, a chimney afire at home raised
a cry in the Fair that Sturt's newspaper shop was afire, and
brought hopeful people crowding to see; occasionally a
loud bang told where some wag had thrown a squib down
into the crowd. But this I never saw. And if I saw, I nowise remember, any of my father's cronies or customers,

any farmer friends, dropping in for a smoke on Fair Day evening, as doubtless they did. Doubtless too I had myself been packed off to bed betimes. The next morning, unless for filth I didn't see, or possibly piles of hurdles from the dismantled pens I didn't notice, nothing was left of the Fair but a smell, mostly of sheep, that clung to the ancient street for a few hours. The quiet of the centuries was recovered. From aloft the Castle looked down as it had done in all my memory, upon a very peaceful town.

CHAPTER XII

STREET SCENES

PEACEFULNESS was in fact the pervading "atmosphere" of Victorian Farnham in spite of an endless change of things interesting to a comfortable urchin. Certainly there was always something going on, something to be noticed. In the slow and spare provincial traffic the long main street furnished a good deal more to look at than horses and carts, dogs and well-known neighbours; and it was generally worth while to stand at the front-room window and watch for something unusual to pass. Once, only once, I saw elephants from a travelling menagerie amble silently though swiftly along the street. More than once that window gave a good point of view of a circus procession— the clowns on their tall stilts striding by almost at one's own level. At that window I was half way up towards the Queen of the Show on her piled-up splendour of gilt and mirrors; could look down on the backs of her pie-bald pony team, on her nonchalant attendants riding hand on hip. If no circus happened to go by there might be a man pushing a "Happy Family." A Happy Family was a wire cage on a long hand-cart, containing all kinds of ill-assorted animals—a dog, a cat, a rabbit, a bird or two— things that one would have expected to be killing one another, and, somehow, seemed to be living together in amity. So at least it looked to a child's sight, staring down upon that interesting medley from the front-room window. The assertion that the animals loved one another explained their being together in one cage.

For some spectacles it was better to be down on the level of the road. On the whole, that was the best place to see even a dancing bear. To be sure, the shaggy docile creature padding along on its chain, behind the uncouth foreign-looking man who had tamed it, might be viewed more safely from upstairs. But the street was too narrow just there for a performance, and it was necessary to join the little crowd further along, to see the bear, immense on his hind legs, dance to the odd singing notes of the keeper with the long stout staff. The "man who played several instruments at once" was more appreciatively watched from the side-walk than from the window; and, as with the bear, need of more room obliged the two or three tumblers—slipping along as if escaped out of the Middle Ages—to choose a wider bit of street before they laid down their strip of carpet and took off their overcoats. The soiled costume—coloured tights and all, revealing well-developed muscles—was justified by the tumbling. Less showy were the occasional sword-swallowers, or the men who carried about with them huge boulders which, for pence, any townsman might smash on their chests with a sledge-hammer also carried about. To carry so heavy a load ought to have been worth something, and was at least harmless; only, these men, being neither of gentle birth, nor rich, ought, ought they not? to have been at work. Lastly, it was well worth while, at the call of toot and drum, to run round any corner to join the ring round Punch and Judy, "seen by us and all the world in circle," and to hear the jovial squeaks of "that sorrowful contumacious captain."

The Front Room was a good place for watching a

"Club!" Many a little public-house had its little benefit society for its own frequenters. If the funds would run to a band, the club members would hire two or three musicians; and hearing a "rub-a-dub" in the distance, it was interesting, and not pathetic, at my then age, to get to the window to see "The Club" go shuffling by. A little pathetic it really was. Should the original members of a club grow too elderly and only too likely to become a drain on the resources, young men would no longer join, so that the older men's attempts at thrift too often failed. And the men showed that they knew it, showed a sort of dis-illusionment in their time-worn faces, as they straggled towards their one day's feast. Straggled. They were too old and too bent to march. They walked, in little forlorn bunches not keeping step; not even keeping any rank; sometimes bent at the knee and hobbling.

In one Club the men stumped along doggedly, wearing their best white smock frocks and chimney-pot hats. This, called "The Round Frock Club," was the same, unless I mistake, as Jack Stone's Club, or "The Dumb Gluttons." At any rate there was one Friendly Society known by this last title, which title was said to have been earned when the club-meeting resolved to hold the annual dinner with-out speeches. Other Clubs were, I think, "The Wheat-sheaf," and "The Red Lion." No doubt there were others too, but with one exception the other names have gone from me.

The one exception was "The Foresters." Even that was threatened, by some apparently nefarious organisation darkly spoken of as "The Oddfellows"; but the Oddfellows I never saw. Not so "The Foresters." These I saw on their feast day, in procession by scores, green-sashed and proud, following their secretary on horseback—he red-faced, moustached, looking a devil of a fellow, with a cavalier hat and, I fancy, a woodman's axe. For was he not leader of "The Foresters"? And is it after all wholly silly if life yields no touch of romance from year's end to year's end, to be one's own playactor for a few hours in the twelve months?

An occurrence that always caused one to pause wherever one happened to be, in the street or at the window, was the clanging of the town-crier's hand-bell. From the end of the Borough the crier himself could often be seen far away "down" East Street, sitting in his room up the steps, in that part of "The Seven Stars" that reaches across to the street; and when he was there the man inspired a touch of fear, as if he might be some unique kind of town constable. But he was all right ringing his bell to call attention. When he began "Lost"—not as if he had any interest in the matter himself, but with loudish declamation, as in a sort of recitative or ritual—of course everybody had to listen. It might be interesting; and anyhow, other mode of advertising there was none. And sometimes you might even make out what had been lost.

The front-room window was pretty good—but the street door of the shop was good too—if soldiers from Aldershot came marching through the town. I will tell of them by and by. Naturally enough one thought small beer of the German Bands, that often took their stand in the street, and whose aching sounds were said to be a sign of rain; and not much better were the local volunteers. It may have handicapped the volunteers that they were recognisable as neighbours—"Lapper" this, Freddie that—when they chose to go in reasonable civilian dress.

On certain days in the month a little crowd would get together, loitering at the foot of Bear Lane; and with luck one might see why they were there. For in due time policemen ("Bobbies") would appear—the Police Station being, then, the building since used as St Polycarp's Church—taking some handcuffed wretch to "The Bench." Later in the day, if the wretch was committed to gaol, a similar crowd would form at likely corners, to see him marched off—nay, it might be half a dozen prisoners in a string—to the railway station, bound for Wandsworth. A solemn sight! Every one viewed it silently. For lighter detentions the local "Lock-up," in "Chokey" in Bear Lane, was enough. One viewed all policemen with a sort of awe; still more, "The Super." That awe seems to point to a working-class ancestry; or it is related to the disquiet I felt, about 1870 or '71 when school inspectors began to be talked about. Would those dreadful persons ever interfere with me? I felt watched, hunted, helpless.

A very different impression remains, which must have been born in my younger years. It puzzles me where to place it; for it shows me a town unlike any other I have in memory—a little quiet summer-evening town—with the townsfolk (some of my own family amongst them) enjoying the air after work. Up and down we sauntered, to and fro under the old houses, on the uneven pitching-stone pavement. There was no hurry, but plenty of time, in balmy evening light. Swallows were wheeling up and down the street; under many eaves their nests could be seen; and though they skimmed so low, we knew, or thought we knew, that that was no sign of rain just then. Rain? Not on that still summer evening. Sometimes someone spoke (not as if it mattered at all) of "The Match"; and once two or three oddly-dressed young men trotted (or may be swiftly walked) in racing shorts, from Aldershot.

Were they, then, The Match? Matches, sometimes called "Lucifers," were little red-headed sticks standing on end, a hundred or more, in a little round box on the table. The lid of the box had a piece of sand-paper pasted on it, for striking the matches. But what had "The Match" along the street to do with all this? Coming from Aldershot, the men might be "officers," and once my sister had not been too clear as to the difference between "officers" and "lucifers"; but that didn't explain the young men trotting in shorts. But it really was unimportant. The swallows were better worth noting; the restful townsfolk, sauntering in the golden evening light, sauntered to such purpose that the delight of it all has lasted for sixty years in my memory.

I dimly fancy that there was more than one "Match"— other young men from Aldershot using that level high-road for a racing track; yet these were not frequent affairs. And if one of them has embalmed as it were a summer evening in my memory, on the other hand autumn and winter afternoons survive as the environment of commoner experiences. And for these colder weather, may be with rain or fog, has driven one indoors and to the front-

room window again. It was from there that I watched
the muffin-man and listened to his hand-bell, admiring
the balance of the tray-full of ware on his head, and
wondering a little, even then, why the man should be
wearing a green apron and why muffins and crumpets had
to be hawked round, when other pastry-cook stuff could
be got at a shop. And then too there was the lamp-lighter.
Not as on summer evenings, after children were in bed,
but in the dusk of every winter afternoon the man might
be seen with his ladder, almost running so as to get done
by dark. Then, it was plain how the phrase "to go like a
lamplighter" had arisen, so tirelessly did the man hurry
from lamp to lamp. It seemed a great improvement when
at last he needed only a long pole with a little sheltered
flame burning in the end, with which he could reach the
gas-lamp and turn it on and light it, all from the pavement.
But, beside each of the old lamps, a short iron bar was at
first provided, for the man to rest his ladder on, so that
he might run up to light the gas by hand. A knife-grinder
sitting at his intricate machine and bending deeply over
his whinny and sparkling emery wheel was good to
watch.

Mention just now of the muffin-man balancing his
tray recalled another sight viewed from that same window
at another season—a man carrying on his head a basketful
of oranges. The odd thing was, that he was obviously
drunk. His legs wobbled; he strayed from side to side of
the street, for there were no motor-cars in those days. But
in vain one hoped to see the downfall of the oranges. Old
David—I think it was Old David—knew all there is to

know about being drunk; and though his legs might wobble the basket was steady enough on his head. He sometimes pushed a coster barrow and sold herrings, strawberries, anything; but most of all I remember his heap of oranges, and his cry, "Orangées, fifty-a-shilling!" echoing down the sunny street. Is "es" a difficult sound for hawkers? Sometimes a little Italian boy would come into the shop, to invite purchase from a tray-full of terra-cotta casts which he called "Imagées."

In my early childhood did I really see my Grandfather (my father's father) standing in Farnham Market beside a plough of his own make as a specimen of his craft, or is it only after hearing about it fairly often that I have come to believe that I saw it myself? One other craftsman I am more sure of having seen similarly engaged in the Market —Old Charlie Bennett, maker of machines—seed-sowing machines, potato-grinders, and so on. Yet even that must be almost before my memory.

Of the market itself so long ago not much lingers. When I was a schoolboy of nine or ten years, the Market-day being on a Thursday and still a school half-holiday then, the old market customs did not seem unfamiliar to me, and likely enough I had known them for years, though I cannot be sure. There, at the lower end of Castle Street, on the paved part just off the Borough, a few head of quiet cattle used to stand, flicking their tails. There, in three or four pens, huddled a few pigs, but no sheep, I think. I knew how a pig should be lifted out of the pen for carrying away, for I often saw some village man clutch a pig up by one ear and hind leg and walk off with it tucked under his arm. Once (it indicates my own height) a pig, so carried, shrieked right into my ear as its new owner passed; and nobody seemed to care but myself, but me it nearly deafened. Sometimes—a sight no motorist may ever see now—the street would be excited by a drove of pigs, wandering or scampering along in front of a man with a long stick—long as a fishing rod—cut from a hedge-row hazel. Nor was it always "in front of" the driver that the opinionated pigs hustled away. I saw then what afterwards I read of in Leigh Hunt—how the driver of pigs was provoked to wail, "They'll run up all manner of streets!" Instead of pigs there might be a little herd of bullocks; or a dozen sheep too swiftly hurried to the butcher's. If what one saw was a cow piteously lowing behind a cart with a calf in it, the day was probably Thursday, the incident being only part of a deal between two farmers at the market; but on other days one might see other sights.

For that was the period when it was still thought no great scandal to see a man or woman drunk, no horror to behold a terrified cur race by with a tin tied to its tail. The gentry set no such high example that common folk need care if cruelty was permitted. So we could look on, even with amusement, when the butcher's sheep (escaping from the butcher boys) leapt high one after the other, all in the same place, and raced away, only to be chased back with huge delight; or when some wretched calf, frightened almost to death, had to be pushed towards the slaughter-house with ingenious twisting of tail. Less obviously cruel, yet probably equally inhumane, was the removal of live

animals in dung cart or farm waggon. Under net drawn
down tight to prevent struggling, the pigs, sheep, calves,
could neither stand nor lie down in comfort, and must have
suffered torments during any long removal.

Our front-room window lent itself famously to looking
down into passing vehicles. These, to be sure, were not
very many. Of course it would be different in these days
of motor-cars; in those days I saw more pigs than gentry.
The latter indeed I hardly looked at, but their horses took
my eye. Often came Captain —'s pair of greys and his
carriage from a near Park; often a beautifully groomed
mouse-coloured cob I called Fennick's. Who Fenwick
was I haven't the least idea; but the glossy animal in the
shafts was a thing to run and look at. Of persons there is
little to be told. From Tilford came, in a little leather
conveyance I afterwards heard called a Booby hutch,
drawn by a large donkey, Miss Strickland, who was said
always to say to her guests "Come and see my white ass!"
Few others can be remembered. There pulled up regularly
at my mother's shop Mr Whatsisname the gentleman
farmer. My mother esteemed him highly for his strong
common sense; and he probably reciprocated. At any
rate, taking *The Times* for himself he used to depre-
cate his further errand, to fetch *The Family Herald* for
his wife, who kept crowds of cats. He drove always in
a high dog-cart which, for the sake of getting good wheels,
he had had built by my father, though my father was no
sort of coach-builder, but a wheelwright. Another cus-
tomer, Mrs Hurt, should be named. Every Saturday she
fetched a number of newspapers for her neighbours in a

village two miles away. Always welcome, not because of the bunch of parsley she brought for a weekly gift, but because it was so pleasant to see her—she was a village woman of a type no longer very common to-day—thick-set and without figure, broad-faced, almost simple with her expression of kindly honesty. She wore a Paisley shawl; looked as if hard work was her hobby that never tired her; and she always had time for a gossip. Fond of reading she was, unlike her son. "Some be rayders," she said, "and some be on-rayders. I be a rayder. Now my son—he's a on-rayder."

One other person may be mentioned as of this period—Old Carrington the astronomer. Curious, by the way, how we called people "Old." I had heard of "Old Cobbett"; I often saw "Old Johnson," the paralytic with trembling hand, only too fascinating; there was "Old Copper," the comfortable wheezy farmer, or "Old Pye." The last named, driving (or perhaps he walked) the two or three miles from Rowledge every Saturday for his weekly paper, was never deterred by a wet day. That, to tell the truth, gave opportunity for working off his standing joke. Wet through, he would say to my mother, "Nasty day for a pie to be out!" But to return to Old Carrington from the Devil's Jumps—reported to live at the bottom of a mysterious hole whence he could see the stars by daylight. Old Carrington was a black-bearded man with eyes that bulged —a consequence, I supposed, of looking at far off things like stars through a telescope. Once (it must have been by some connivance with his coachman) I got inside the brougham where I had often seen the astronomer smoking a cigar, and the floor of the brougham was half an inch or more deep in cigar ash. His disappearance, after some family scandal, interested me not at all.

I used to run little errands for my mother. Once I was sent to a bakehouse (long since demolished) in East Street, to fetch our Sunday cake. This was on a Sunday morning. What can have been the occasion? My mother was not a Sabbatarian; but she would not willingly have had me ignore the commandment. For years I thought it wrong to run on a Sunday.

Once there came to 18 Borough a soldier (or so I thought him) who stalked inquisitively through to the very back premises. He was conducting the first Ordnance Survey. More than once—indeed fairly often—a couple of soldiers with papers in their hands and probably on horseback, would search out the public-houses in the little town, looking bothered. In fact they were "billeting"; and in due course a battery or two of artillery came rattling in, and turned up Castle Street. An hour or two later soldiers leading horses in loose harness went jogging off one or two at a time this way or that. And at nightfall you might see at one side of Castle Street guns parked in order, a sentry marching to and fro beside them; while along the streets soldiers were lounging. Next morning by break-fast time the horses would jingle back towards Castle Street; then came a further marching and rumbling; and by noon nothing more was seen of the artillery.

To set off against this suggestion of national order, came only too often a suggestion of the impoverishment of public resourcefulness, and general indifference to it.

Street singers (mentioned before) were an almost daily experience. They all looked wretched—perhaps that was their cue. Sometimes they bawled out long wailing hymns; now and then a whole family draggled miserably along the street—man, woman, and neglected children; and once a little gang of men limped along, singing "We áre poor labourers out of work, And we've got no work to do."

Two functionaries, meanwhile preserved in Farnham a hint of eighteenth-century economy. Mr Lovelock, the milkman (our milkman at least—if there were others I never noticed them), brought milk into the town from about a mile and a half away. His cows, or the farmer's cows that supplied him, were probably farther off still; but a mile and a half was practically the distance between our shop and Mr Lovelock's cottage at Passmore Bridge. A shortish stocky man, very respectable in pepper-and-salt suit, he walked rather ponderously, as well he might. For he had no truck or hand-cart. He carried the milk on a yoke across his shoulders—carried it in two shining pails hanging one at each side. No doubt he had a hoop or frame to keep the pails spread away from his knees, and chains hanging down from the yoke[1], but I remember none of this. I only remember Mr Lovelock's good-tempered down-looking walk, unhasting and unresting, loaded with the heavy cans. He came regularly every afternoon; perhaps every morning; and I think he had no holiday for years.

[1] A yoke ought to be preserved in our provincial museums. It involved a clever bit of woodwork by local carpenters. Along with a yoke should be a butcher-boy's tray, a butter mould, a chimney sweep's bat, a wooden bucket.

In passing, notice should be taken of the proper way of carrying water or milk in a pail. In fact it is rather easier to carry two pails than one, for the sake of balance; but in either case it is well to have something to keep the pail from knocking against your knee and splashing you. In my childhood people used a girl's wooden hoop for this. There was a public pump close by—a cast iron pump (I never knew where the water it yielded came from) in that wide bit of street at the foot of Bear Lane; and many people came to it for water. These people generally brought hoops. A hoop laid on two pails (between the handles of them) did not add appreciably to the weight, and, keeping them apart, made a space to walk in. Nothing could be more convenient.

The other piece of eighteenth-century economy was the purveying of water by "Old Tom," to people who had no well and could not go to the pump. But this should not be crowded in at the end of too long a chapter. Let me start afresh.

CHAPTER XIII

OLD TOM

THERE was a well at 18 Borough; at 83 East Street a furlong away there was another; I knew of several between
these two, and no doubt there were many more. For this
street (antiquarians might do worse than consider the
matter if the site of the town in its remotest origin is of any
interest to them)—this street being part of the Pilgrim's
Way, and of the main road westwards from London to
Winchester—being also parallel between the stream on
its south and the ancient track (since followed by Farnham
Park Avenue) half a mile to the north of it, this street seems
to have been determined in its course by the change from
the meadow-lands to the steeper uplands beside them.
Just there, all along the edge of the chalk, water could be
easily got—where the chalk leaves off and the meadow
clay begins. And just there, it may be suspected, the very
earliest settlement made the nucleus of the present street,
water being so handy.

But if few people along that bit of ancient Farnham
needed more water than they could dip or pump from their
own wells, these few were not the only townsfolk. Others
elsewhere wanted water. Unfortunately for them, the
River was "a bit off" with their own sewage. However,
yet another supply in due time could be tapped. High over
the town, on a knob of a chalk hill, stood Farnham Castle.
Whether or no its site was a prehistoric "camp," as they
say, is unimportant here. Ages before my time water had
been collected near the Castle perhaps from Hungry Hill

a mile to the north, and was stored in a huge tank in the same chalk knob on which the Castle itself stood. And some Bishop, Lord of the Manor of Farnham, had made this same supply available for his people in the town. To effect this, the great tank just outside his Castle gates had been connected with a "conduit" leading to a pump at the bottom of Castle Street, where that street butts into the main west road.

But now note. The road down into the town from the Castle sags—drops steeply—like a loose clothes line down a hill side; and under the road the unseen conduit must sag too. And immediately after its very first descent, Castle Steps being now left behind and Castle Street lying still out of sight lower down round the corner, something queer happens to the conduit. I never saw it indeed; but, under the grassy bank beside the road the conduit comes to some sort of chamber or pool. And if I didn't see, I heard—heard a boom as from an empty room, when I threw a stone at the battered door visible enough at that time, in the sloping grass at the road-side. The unseen hollow boomed.

What was it within there? The door, some two feet square, had round it a little brick-work, and was surmounted by a dilapidated stone panel (since removed and built into the Castle Wall) carved with a mitre—the sign of some long-forgotten bishop. And though for the most part the door was locked, so that I never saw what was behind it, there were times when, from a safe distance away, I saw it opened.

"From a safe distance away." For "Old Tom," whom

I loved to watch, was there getting water. He baled it out (with a ladle on a pole) from the dark place behind the door, to fill a water-barrel he had wheeled up from the town on a low four-wheeled hand-cart. Having filled his barrel, he locked the conduit door and trundled back down Castle Street to deliver his water, while I could pelt the door in safety. A penny, or perhaps a halfpenny, a bucket was Old Tom's price, but I have been told that he had regular customers. The singular thing is that this was not his own enterprise after all. He was an employed man, working for one of the shop-keepers.

That I didn't know, or at any rate I didn't care about it, at the time. I used to watch for Old Tom to lock the conduit door and trundle off with his load, and then a stone —the biggest I could heave—thrown at the door produced the hollow booming I wanted. I am told now that he was "an obstinate old devil," Old Tom; that boys, by cruel pranks, delighted to make him chase them. But none of this is what I remember. What I do get, thinking of Old Tom, is a notable feeling of having lived in the eighteenth century. It may be due to his queer antique figure; his dark slate-coloured smock-frock, his bent walk, his hair in want of cutting; or it may be that some special scene survives round my memory of him. In memory it seems a rainy afternoon, yet a glint of sunlight suddenly glistens along the wet street. The street too, antique enough and gloomy enough, is very quiet, and Old Tom of the water-truck is slowly making his bent-backed way up the steps to a dingy tenement that looks as if it had been there, squeezed into East Street, for centuries. There is nothing modern in that memory. Grimy street and dingy brick-work, leisurely town, obstinate old man in smock-frock, and antiquated task—it all would do very well for my idea of the times of Dr Johnson.

The conduit ended at the lower corner of Castle Street, in what is now the Town Hall Buildings, where, not so many years ago, I saw a man pumping water. I wonder how he had got permission, or from whom? In Old Tom's time the control of this pump, as of the conduit I have told of, was vested, as I said, in one of the Farnham trades-men. I have never found out how the right was got, as it must have been, from the Bishop.

There was a shoe shop in the same building with "The Bush," and I can still picture the owner—a heavy man, with a limp when he moved—standing in his shop door-way to look out into the Borough. But what leading shop-keeper in these days would wear, as he did, a white apron and bib, proclaiming himself too habitually a practical workman? His wife, kind-eyed, had her largish flattish face thickly pitted by small-pox.

That is a thing rarely seen now, but it was only too common in my childhood. Club-feet were frequent; and wooden legs; and arms ending in hooks instead of hands. I once saw a milkman (rival probably to Old Lovelock), whose hook looked very convenient for carrying a pail of milk. Some people, with easily dazzled sight, went about with green shades. I am surprised, now, at the number of men I seem to have seen said to have been sailors, and cer-tainly wearing ear-rings, to strengthen their eyes it was alleged.

128

Although I have no recollection of ever feeling bored—how should one be bored amid so many sights?—two or three other things have left such a mark on my memory that a usual lack of excitement may be suspected. One of these more exciting things was the performance of a stage play by some marionettes. Their tent was somewhere about where the present football ground is, near to the Brewery; and I hope I shall never forget the rapid wooden jerk of those little strutting figures which impressed me so much at the time. I cannot "place" the affair at all. It was the first stage-play I ever witnessed—with the exception, perhaps, of Punch; and I never saw marionettes again, save dancing dolls on a street barrow many years afterwards. My brother says he went too. That may be. I for my part cannot remember ever entering the tent or leaving it. All that remains to me is a sort of tinted streak of memory—a little green plush figure stamping across a dim stage, and possibly, a voice mouthing something! yet it is rather pleasant to recover even that tinted streak in the fog of the far past. Evidently I must have enjoyed life keenly, that afternoon.

One other memory, almost as vague, discovers me looking at the beasts in a travelling menagerie ("me-nadgery" we called it)—probably Wombwell's. This can certainly be "placed" to this extent—it must have been after "The New Road" had been opened. For it was in a certain corner of The New Road—now built over with shops that themselves begin to look ancient—that the menagerie was pitched. But what did I see there? It would be easier to say what I smelt there! For I still shrink with dislike from the memory of a strong smell of "carbolic" associated with the Wild Beast Show. That smell was a new thing to me then. I attributed it to the strange animals; though now I know what it must have been, and can guess that the sawdust strewn over the meadow grass had been well mixed with disinfectant powder. As for the animals—there *may* have been a mandril—a vague memory of blue and red (?) lines of fur against an ape's muzzle persuades me that I must have seen some curious ape—but the only animals I recall with certainty were a couple of half-grown giraffes. Eight feet high they may have stood, but at any rate it was satisfying to see that giraffes really had long necks. For the rest—were there any quaggas, zebras? There was something stripy, not a tiger. Undoubtedly there were piles of cages; for when I came to read "Peter Simple" years afterwards I seemed to have had experience of the menagerie which figures in that book. The mental pictures to illustrate it were all there.

One summer afternoon (probably June) people gathered in a little crowd (there being no hurry of motor-cars then to make the place dangerous) just where South Street joins The Borough. They were looking up with leisurely excitement, as if they had all the afternoon to spare, at a swarm of bees buzzing round a chimney there. By and by a man came with a ladder and hived the swarm—and that's that. But I like to think how peaceful the little town must have been then. The fancy of its great quiet fits in very well with other fancies—especially, at this moment, of the serenity which allowed a little boy like me to toddle off

without a qualm to the barber's. In fact I recall two bar-
bers. One of them—a Yankee, I think he was—amused
his customers, or at least he amused me—by doing little
conjuring tricks on the floor of his tiny shop. Why not?
Nobody was in any hurry. In after years, waiting to have
one's hair cut was a tedious waste of time; but perhaps it
would have been otherwise, if the man had left off in the
middle of cutting your hair, to play some queer trick with
—I cannot remember what—on the floor of his saloon.

But I must have been even more of an infant when I
went to the other barber's; though that, to be sure, was a
little farther away, and even across the street, now so
dangerously full of rushing traffic. It was safe enough
then. No doubt at first I had my brother to take care of
me. I infer it from a dim memory of having his hand to
take hold of, while a black-avised sort of fellow cut my hair.
But at last a time came when the same black-avised fellow
did not command me to sit in the tall baby-chair that would
lift me up nearer to his reach, but was content to have me
in an ordinary chair. I was content too. Oh! but I felt a
man! And while I am not sure that anybody was with me,
I feel sure enough that there was no danger as I went
home. It was perfectly safe to leave a little chap to cross
the road alone, when the ordinary days were so quiet—the
winter days, no less than that summer day when bees
swarmed over the house roof. I remember the naked gas-
jet in the barber's shop; the street grimily luminous from
the shop windows; the sunny sitting-room "indoors" at
home. I don't remember any globe over the sitting-room
gas-jet; but I do remember the curly ended gas pendant—

offensively covered with house flies at certain seasons, until more offensive "catch-em-alive" papers were brought in, or hideous sticky strings hung down from the ceiling! It must have been autumn when those glass traps—baited with beer and sugar—were stood about in the rooms, for wasps were caught—through the glass their struggles amongst drowning flies could be watched. (One often saw wasps and flies at the sugar in grocers' shop-windows.) I had no pity for flies in those days. In fact I was cruel. I did horrid things (my mother never knew) that need not be described now. For, in those days I could move hands and fingers fast enough to catch a fly.

CHAPTER XIV

SUPERSTITIONS

WE had comical ideas about health, or perhaps it would be better to say No ideas at all. I have told how I was taken to see a man lying in a stupor of small-pox. Of course modern precautions against disease were unknown. People often could be seen with respirators. Tubercular consumption was called "a Decline." If measles broke out in a family, it was mere common sense to let all the children sleep in the same bed together, for there was no avoiding this trouble, and to have it all over and done with at once was a saving of the mother's time in the end. The same reasoning applied to scarlatina. As for whooping cough, it could not be got rid of until May, but then it was sure to go. I never heard of chicken-pox, or of German measles; quite possibly one or other of these ailments was what we called simply "a rash," which would disappear after a day or two if left alone. Although in the silly game, Punch was said to have died "in a fit," and it was asked "What sort of a fit?" no discrimination was ever really attempted. Only "a fit" was a nasty dangerous thing. If you dropped dead "in a fit" you would be "brought home on a shutter," as there was no ambulance, but every shop had shutters. Dangerous it was, too, to cut your hand between finger and thumb, that being a sure way to get lockjaw. If, when a tooth came out, you neglected to show it to your father or mother, it was only too likely to be replaced by a dog-tooth. To have an eye-tooth pulled out

133

might be very bad for the eyes. A good way to get rid of a loose tooth was to tie it with cotton to the window-fastening; then get somebody to go outside and dash a bucket of water at the window. Involuntarily you recoiled; and when you recovered, you found that the tooth was hanging on the cotton, clear of your gum. But who troubled about teeth in those days? To go to a dentist was almost unheard of. There were no anaesthetics—you might as well suffer the decay of teeth as the certain agonies of dentistry, for which moreover the professional charges were quite beyond the reach of the humbler shopkeepers like my father and mother. To a large extent this applied to the medical profession all round. You took risks, for it cost too much to go to a doctor. You took powders too! True, my father set his face against the practice. But one had grandmothers also; and there were convenient doses to be got at a grocer's—senna, rhubarb, camomile, Stedman's powders, and a loathsome brown powder we called "Grandmother's powder" which we hated—fortunately, for it contained some form of mercury.

A certain danger attended grimacing—you might "get fixed so" by a malicious Fate, and it would be awful! Distressing indeed were some of the prospects one faced. I once pushed a finger through the hole in the arm of a baby chair, and for an agonised half-minute faced the expectation of wearing that chair for the rest of my life. Rings (what rings can they have been?) too often got alarmingly fixed below my finger joint, and there was disquieting talk of soaping the finger to get the ring off. Yes, that was disquieting. What if the soap should fail? It was dangerous to chew string or to bite cotton instead of taking scissors to it, for, if swallowed, string or cotton might wind round your heart and kill you. Not dangerous was it but truly painful to swallow a large sweet too soon. As it lay melting, the dull ache across your chest was aggravated by the thought how nice the sweet would have been between the teeth. For in those days one's teeth were strong enough to crack a nut; and it was sheer delight to scrunch up a sweet. You could bite the end off a twisted sugar-stick or a plait of barley-sugar; there was only a little risk of getting your jaws fixed uncomfortably in a piece of liquorice; but the really tiresome thing was one of the large square acid-drops. The smaller round sort, which got damp and clogged together in their little paper bags, were as safe to suck as they were nice; so were their sister pear-drops and raspberry-drops. Bull's eyes—those magically streaked peppermint bull's eyes—never misbehaved; no lump of sugar-candy got stuck in one's gullet; cakes of "hard-bake," thick with white almonds, were at worst no worse than "stick-jaw"; but the large square acid-drops only too often slid down before one knew; and then their square corners hurt like anything. By the way, at Farnham Fair we used to get, in a little twist of paper (do you know how to twist up paper into a small bag?) a handful of those tiny sweets called "Hundreds and Thousands," that melted on the tongue like dust of sugar.

Chilblains might be cured by thrashing them with holly until they bled—so at least I was told. Being never much troubled with the disorder (and having no courage either) I never tried the remedy but was content to take it on trust. For nettle-stings (I did have my share of them) it was supposed to be good, though it never seemed in my experience much good, to lay a dock leaf on the sting.

We had a wholesome dread of all berries from the hedge. Haws indeed I ate (they had a foul name), though despising, even in those unsophisticated years, the thin layer of fruit round the comparatively immense stone; but I chanced no other wild fruit, save blackberries. For a certain name frightened me, Deadly Nightshade. I did not actually know the Deadly Nightshade. I am not sure even now that I have ever seen it; but the name was awful enough. It scared me not only from the privet and barberry and other black and blue fruits which might be "deadly" for all I knew; it also joined forces with another scare-word—"poison"—to make me shy of scarlet haws, vermilion "Lords and Ladies," and other beautiful things, some of which doubtless may not have been good to eat, but all of which were "poison" in my belief. Apparently I feared death: it is not clear why. Worms that had been mangled under the spade were thought to die and escape their agony, but not before night.

In this connection an odd thought occurs to me. We had no country "charms," no rural lore at all, though my mother had been born and brought up in a farm-house and, while I was a little child, had her sister, another country girl, to help her. The sister, it is true, had a few sayings probably of rural origin. Thus she conveyed to us, no doubt from the bake-house at her home, the name "kissing crust" for the pale just crisped crust of bread: a "lollipop" for the sweet brown syrup that sometimes was baked on the end of an apple-turnover or "apple-crowdin." But I got from nowhere any of the local country superstitions, and the reason was almost certainly that my mother's own mother had a strong religious disapproval of such ideas. I never heard of fairies as if they were anything real; or of ghosts, or spirits, or omens. So a religious sentiment came passing down the generations in our family; and, reaching me, saved me, for one (others in my family were not so fortunate) a good deal of real anguish. For, when at last I came to hear of ghosts, not believing in them, I was pleasantly excited; prophesies of the approaching end of the world did not affect me much[1], nor was I much worried by the Last Judgment. Years afterwards it did indeed disturb me a little. When I cried to myself "I don't believe in God"; and when promptly I said to myself "You'll go to Hell for it," the unreason of that rejoinder did not strike me. But, all this searching of the heart having occurred one winter evening in a dark room, the dreadful plight I was in was forgotten as soon as I got back into gaslight where people were talking, with ordinary life going on.

While my mother, I have no doubt of it, never got very far away from a tender and tolerant piety, talking little, but self-sacrificing and devout and fearless; my father was, I think, more ready to be amused and open-minded. He was indeed very orthodox, but there was a good deal of

[1] Perhaps I thought "If it is so; we can't help it." That, at any rate, was my father's rejoinder some years later, when my mother expressed horror at the idea that men had descended from monkeys. My father smiled sadly: it seemed a pity but we couldn't help it.

obstinacy in his orthodoxy. Like his own father [1] before him, he seemed willing to leave the clergy alone. Yet when a new rector of Farnham preached in a white surplice instead of in a black gown, the innovation called up all my father's stubbornness, and as a protest he walked off every Sunday morning to Hale Church, a mile away. I am not aware that he ever entered Farnham Parish Church again; yet he was probably more regular in his opposition to the new rector than he had ever troubled to be in support of the old. I don't believe that in his inmost heart he really cared a straw about Darwin's theory or anything of the sort. He was only interested to know; and, being a voracious reader, he read everything he could get hold of.

In raking together these memories, I have recalled a few words and phrases that do not belong, but may as well not be lost. For instance, there was a little thrill in answering "No!" to the question, asked with bated breath, "Are you afraid of Neverwags?" You felt brave, knowing very well all the time that a "Neverwag" was nothing more awful than an ordinary piece of furniture—table or bed— that never moved. It was similarly amusingly dreadful to be threatened after any slight calamity such as swallowing an acid-drop, "You're sure to die after it." Going upstairs to bed was "Going up Wooden Hill to Bedfordshire." To be arrested by a policemen and taken to the lock-up was "to be pulled up." The attempted rhyme "See a pin and pick it up All the day you'll have good luck," was at least

---

[1] His own father, old George Sturt the wheelwright, contemporary and fellow-townsman of Cobbett, had no quarrel, that I ever heard of, with the clergy; but he refused to be visited by any clergyman in his old age.

in favour of tidiness. I never saw anything even funny in the question "How many beans make five?" nor did I ever hear that there was any impropriety hidden in it— or anything comic when my elder sister, holding up some large needle or other, remarked fiercely "Sword enough to kill ye." No less futile was the observation "Good old iron, never rusts," which I knew to be false. When one was in a passion of impatience, it was exasperating to be asked, "Have it now? or wait till you get it?" And if you wanted something that could not be had, it made you cross, though you might know it to be true, to be answered "Then Want must be your Master."

Infantile games too recurred—"Put your finger in the fox's hole," "Chop-nose day," "My mother made a pudding about so long," "Pease pudding hot," not forgetting "This little pig went to market"—that widespread expression of a mother's happiness in her child. This indeed I had thought of often during the war, which seemed only the more shameful, as I wondered if any English mother could delight in her baby's toes in the time of the Zeppelin raids, or German mothers could enjoy such happiness during the occupation of the Ruhr or Cologne. The old rhyme, "Baby, baby he's a giant," somehow made the famous military officers—English, French, German alike—look silly, in their portraits in the daily papers, they seemed so determined to be stern and look ruthless.

An early example of modern advertising—the one word "Ozokerit" appearing, without any explanation, on all the hoardings—did its duty by attracting attention. The fancy pronunciation folk tried ("Oozy-carrot," for instance) did not clear up the mystery yet served the advertiser's ends, familiarising us with the name of his new brand of candles in due time disclosed.

To this period or a little earlier belong the names of two music-hall songs—"Champagne Charley" and "Slap Bang." I cannot even guess how I came by them at all; but words and tunes, half-forgotten now, were as well known to me as "Pop goes the weasel"—a contemporary more recently revived.

CHAPTER XV

ROUND AND ABOUT THE TOWN

On Sunday afternoons we had dessert—an apple perhaps, that one could hang by the stem to roast before the bars of the sitting-room fire (and ah! how it sputtered, when the juice came guttering out); or an orange, or two or three plums, or a few cherries, or even half a dozen straw-berries. There were never nearly enough strawberries for my appetite; but what could be done when a small plateful cost money, and there were six or seven people to help eat it?

My father and mother, glad of the day's rest, spent those Sunday afternoons upstairs in the Front Room, dozing a good deal; and that they might be the quieter, we children were packed off downstairs, in charge of Eliza, the maid-of-all-work—hardly more than a child herself, but ex-pected (as is the fate of working-class girls) to show a little steadier common-sense than other children.

Eliza (the hired girl usually had that name bestowed on her, if it was not already her own) was willing enough, so far as I know to romp with us, or to chatter. It seems to me I owe to one of the Elizas on one of these Sunday afternoons a certain "startler," too good to be forgotten. It began in a sepulchral undertone, telling how a girl, having a mistress with a golden arm, stole the arm when her mistress died. And at night, going to bed, the girl saw that a certain cupboard door was open. (I knew that door very well. It was in the corner of a bedroom I sometimes slept in, at my grandmother's at Farnborough—a black door in a shadowy corner.) So, the door being open, the girl shut it. It opened again, and she shut it and locked it. It opened again and out walked her mistress's skeleton. "Where's your beautiful bright blue eyes?" the girl asked. "All mouldered away and gone," said the skeleton, in a low and measured graveyard voice.

> "Where's your beautiful flaxen hair?"
> "All mouldered away and gone."
> "Where's your beautiful golden arm?"

"YOU GOT IT! YOU GOT IT!" This in sudden scream to make you jump.

Many a Sunday afternoon I went to church, no doubt taken by Eliza. I preferred "Sacrament Sundays," once a month; because after "sacrament" the priest, easing off a little then, spared us the long and dreary Litany, as already told, and let us off with the shorter Evening Prayers. Only, too often (also told before) another tiresome hindrance delayed one's getting out of church to breathe freely and chatter if one wanted to. Some wretched "Christening" had to be gone through. And on the whole it was insufficient compensation to be allowed to kneel up in one's pew and face round towards the Font. Still the Baptism lasted too long and one couldn't go home until nearly tea-time.

One Sunday afternoon stands apart in my memory. Probably it was no unusual thing for Eliza to take us for a walk in nice weather instead of to church; but the only walk of the kind that I remember at all was this eventful one. We were passing up Hoghatch ("Hogidge") Lane,

142

outside of Farnham Park. In the Park itself there are two "Swallow-holes," where tiny streamlets from higher up the hill disappear under the chalk; and to the westwards, outside the Park, the same sort of thing happens. From the footpath of the pasture we were crossing, we could see what looked like a dry pond down in a hollow not half a furlong away. We didn't know it might be a sort of slough. There was no water; no grass either; nothing but a smooth and reddish-yellow surface. As soon as I could run to it I tried to cross that surface; and then—my feet promptly began sinking into sticky clay. Did I scream? Did I struggle? I cannot say now. I have a vague recollection of somebody hauling me out on to firm earth (it was probably my brother; you want help like his, as I know, if you are in a hole) but the next thing I seem to see with any vividness of memory is a little group of us disconsolately walking down Castle Street that Sunday afternoon, our walk spoilt and myself with boots so plastered with clay it was a shame to be seen in them on a Sunday. (Perhaps that was the death of my concern about appearances. I never cared about clothes in later life.) Did I get a scolding, or did Eliza? As far as can be guessed now, the one to suffer most from that disastrous homecoming would be my mother, who, an hour earlier, must have been at pains to get me decently dressed.

Probably my walks had not at that early age extended much farther than to the scene of that Sunday afternoon mishap. Yet I must have been used enough to going as far as that. For instance, there was the Pound, a little beyond the second Park stile. It must have been familiar;

for I do not remember having waited that day to look into the Pound—tucked into a corner of the Park fence. Certainly it was no new thing to me. I had seen animals in the Pound—locked in, I used to think indignantly, for punishment; for I hardly knew then that a horse or a cow or a donkey was property, and I had not the least idea of a Lord of the Manor interested in strayed animals. But I knew of the Pound well within my walks, even as I knew of the Turnpike Gates just beyond the town—one of them round the corner, past Castle Steps; the other down the Guildford Road, placed so as to secure tolls from the big waggons from Bourne Mill. Once more, I cannot have been very old, that day when I heard with wonder of my brother's walk to Crooksbury Hill. Such a height! Was it as high as a house, I asked, naming the highest thing I could think of. My brother's answer has gone from my memory; but I can recall where this talk took place—atop of the ladder into the loft over the coal-hole—well enough to satisfy me now that I really did feel it hard to believe that any hill—even Crooksbury—could be as high as a house.

Other walks of about that period stick in my memory. One time we went across to a farm-house—probably the bailiff's at Aldershot Park. There, a courtyard not only contained a horse-chestnut tree but was strewn with fallen chestnuts! What bliss! I felt I wanted nothing more than to have a chestnut tree of my own; and even years afterwards was hardly prepared for the disillusionment of possession. Can it have been that in the autumn years afterwards the sunshine was less golden, the afternoon less richly serene, than in the quiet courtyard at Aldershot Park, in my childhood?

In those same years I grew familiar with street things, some of which interest me more now than they did then. What, I wonder, was the meaning of two or three tottery and green-mouldy posts in Downing Street? There was one—it was hollow at the top—standing well out on the edge of the pavement in the ascent where Downing Street joins the Borough; and there were one or two others round the corner lower down, across the road opposite the Hop Bag. What were they? Inconvenient even then and even in that old rugged pavement, of course they eventually had to be removed; but I have a notion that with their removal went almost the last[1] suggestion that this street had once been meadow-land, needing fences or boundaries of which these posts were a decrepit relic. The old Farnham of my childhood was, to be sure, not far from being still the agricultural centre it was centuries ago.

Still the old streets were very quiet. Long afterwards, I was able to play marbles in the gutters; and one had to walk warily for fear not, as now, of careless motorists but of dog messes on the kerb. I learnt then to expect rain when I saw swallows flying low along the street (to be sure, I sometimes fancied at a later date that the horse-droppings might have something to do with their low flight), and the rainy colour of the street in my memory seems to justify the forecast. No such aspect, but the peacefulness of warm

[1] One thing remains to this day. The name "Longbridge" can point to nothing else than a wooden foot-bridge over the stream, to join Abbey Street to the town, too often cut off by flood.

summer, rewards a fancied glance up at swallow-nests clustered under eaves over the street. I am going along the old pavement—a spatter of white spots causes me to look up; and there they are—the mud nests, the busy birds. There is no mud fit for them now, but there are few birds, I am told.

At the end of West Street it annoyed me, one day, to see, over an old smithy, the name of some man unknown to me, as "Wheelwright." But was not my father a wheel-wright? What right had anybody else to practise his trade?

In the opposite direction I got sometimes as far as to Bourne Mill—past White Post, and the carpenter's shop, even past the Turnpike Gate and the funny little man with the black hair and the high-pitched voice who kept the gate. Before you were old enough to go on to Moor Park, or even to Covett's Coppice[1] with its fascinating stream, you came to Bourne Mill. And that in itself was a Place and no mistake! Indeed I'd like to see it again; again to see the summer afternoon and the warm blue sky against the tiles—the many cornered old roof with pigeons and sunny slopes and shady nooks. There was a little leaden drinking cup hanging from a chain, and a brass knob you pushed (much as you press the "push" of an electric bell, only this was larger) to get water from the near tap. Old Mr Simmonds plainly had pity for thirsty wayfarers; and I, if not exactly thirsty, liked to drink if the day was hot and the road dusty, so as to taste the weather the better. Then there was a little sloping orchard, scarce hidden by

[1] Now the site of the town Sewage Farm.

an ancient and probably dying thorn hedge. A shadowy lane rose steeply beside it; you had to push through a creaky wicket gate first. And from the shadow, you could see half hidden in darkness of trees a waterfall—the wonderfall that worked the mill. It was worth while to wait a long time there, watching and listening. Yet, best of all, giving to Bourne Mill a glamour all its own, you might see a peacock. In fact, I rather think there was more than one at Bourne Mill. And not always, but with good luck, you might see a stately bird, even with its tail spread and splendid, on the wall opposite the mill, across the road. There was always a chance too, if but a small chance, that in the road could be picked up a peacock's feather. Verily it was worth while to be big enough to walk past Bourne Mill.

CHAPTER XVI

PLAY

I

In my memory, Farnham saunters its way into an easygoing and sleepy old provincial town, clean-aired yet dingy for want of paint. I have spoken of playing marbles along the gutter by the roadside. The game, called "splits," or "follows," was played by two boys, shooting alternately each at the other's marble, the first shot being from one marble to the other after the two had been dropped on the ground together (one atop of the other) and had rolled apart. A game very like "Follows," called "Bonce," we played with big pebbles, hurling them (not "shooting" them) one after the other along country roads, where you met no one at all. You went fast and far, that way. For "Follows" it was quiet enough in the streets, people walking on the pavement being no hindrance to your game in the gutter. Nor yet was the steady-going horse traffic in the roadway often a hindrance.

In many places a little hole was scooped out with finger-tips against a wall for the game of "Auntie" (or was it perhaps Anti?). I have never played at Auntie but have often seen little groups of excited and shouting urchins so intent on it that ordinary townsfolk had to pass round outside them on the sidewalk. If out of four or five marbles tossed all together one or more stayed in the hole it meant something that caused the players to shout and skip and wear an expression of little devils. And I have a nasty feeling that it was sheer snobbishness that kept me from

148

playing; for was not Auntie a game for the lower orders—
the ragged and the grimy? But perhaps it was dislike of
gambling. At the Grammar School, "Bird in the Bush"
—a fine gambling game with marbles—never had any
attractions for me; I cared too little about winning. In a
race with another boy down the middle of the street, it was
not a motor-car, or even a farm-cart, that induced me to
slow down, but a precocious realisation that being first
didn't matter to me very much. In marbles the truly respectable game was "Shoot-ring" or "Ring-taw." My
father showed me how to shoot a marble off my thumb;
one scarce needed showing the meaning of "Knuckle-
down" or of "Brish," or of "No knocks away!" A "taw"
was a marble used for shooting; and an "alley" or "alley-
taw" was not so very different. Of course nobody would
dream of using an "alley" as an ordinary marble, one of
the small and common sort. It could only be a "taw";
and, come to think of it, an alley was a little larger than a
mere marble. A "blood-alley" was white with veinings
of red, and was much prized. Other taws were made of
glass; but common little marbles—brown, buff, blue—
looked as cheap as the rubbish from a stonemason's yard,
or even as if they had been moulded in a clay pit.

Tops were rather a doubtful joy to me. I do not mean
humming-tops—those beautiful hollow wooden things,
pale painted and varnished, showing a gaudy landscape.
These, held steady with a special handle, could be spun
at one's leisure and were sure to hum. A metal variant of
the humming top, spun in the same way, could be supplied
with bent wires which it whirled round very prettily and

for a longish time before it "died." Or, there were tiny tops to spin between thumb and finger. The praise I got for doing this well made me fond of these diminutive things. And then there were teetotums. But peg-tops were a trial to me. At school there was a game—a circle about a yard in diameter was scratched in the dust; and in that circle boys spun their tops (if they could!) while other boys hurled down theirs, all spinning, in the hope of striking the revolving peg into somebody else's top. The bother of it was, that mine never would spin! It fell into the ring, a dead lump, for other boys to jeer at and try to spoil. I did not like that game, and seldom even tried to play it.

What was the error? To this day I do not know. As I was left-handed, I have tried to believe that a change of hands at the critical moment may have been the cause of failure. But then, the little peg-tops called French tops (I had one, painted green) would always spin all right, thrown "underhand"; but I was ashamed to be so "girlish." None the less, the proper "manly" throw from the shoulder downwards (and that was the only way to damage somebody else's top) could never be achieved. I chewed my whip-cord very wet; wound it very tight round the top; held it carefully with the brass button (soldier's uniform button) at the back of middle and third finger; and threw—and there lay the top on the ground, with no spin in it! Oh! it was disappointing after so much trouble. Indeed I deserved well. (I have spent hours with a string whip, whipping a whip-top or a hollow "gig.") Properly spun a peg-top could be lifted from the ground on to the palm of the hand, spinning all the time. A top going round so fast that it did not sway at all was said to be "gone to sleep."

Better than tops were hoops; boys' hoops. (I scorned girls' wooden hoops.) A hoop for a boy was about eighteen to thirty inches in diameter, made of light rod-iron. (Mine, of course, was made at my father's—afterwards my own—smithy, where I could watch the whole process—could see the rod bent, the ends "shut" and all. And sometimes some other urchin would bring a broken hoop to be mended there. It was all good to see. I liked to watch Will Hammond or Porter at work. I was able to get good hard hoop-sticks—oak or ash. And a good stick was necessary, for your hoop was a sort of steed that would not go without walloping. If you beat hard and often it not only went fast, but the fine ringing of the iron was an entrancing tune to run to. And so you whacked and whacked, until sometimes the hoop broke and had to be taken to the blacksmith. A good hoop-stick of course was useful for guiding the hoop too; could be used as a break; and was in short the only tool with which a self-respecting boy could be seen "trolling" a hoop. I despised the boys who "scaled" their hoops, with iron hooks. The milksops! And what freedom could an unhappy hoop enjoy (and hoops were live things) held in with a hook in its driver's hand? A hoop in front of a hoop-stick would bound and run—run away from you, down a hill if you were not a good driver. And there was a way of tossing it forwards so that it seemed to scamper back behind you—oh, it was fine to be a boy with a hoop!

On a cold winter day you could get warm, and keep

warm running beside that companion. In a sharp frost, not only did it sound well as the stick threshed and threshed upon the iron. More than that, the hoop (tiresome in mud) ran with spirit over the ruts of a frozen road. Roads were not then as now, tarred and smooth. They were not even rolled! For a week or two together after the new gravel (that was the local road-metal round about Farnham) had been spread on them, and in fact until it had been worn in, the roads were unfit, but afterwards Farnham roads were better for hoops than Farnham pavements. For the latter were cobbled with ironstone (save for a short yet delightful stretch in Castle Street of smooth Portland Stone) and the hoop went over them "with a cheerful bumpy sound" a little wearisome. Fortunately the roadway was safe. Best of all perhaps were the hop-ground paths. These, where no traffic but foot traffic came, were smooth enough, and gave miles in which you could troll your hoop.

For boys those hop-grounds and paths provided a play-ground just after hop-picking and all through the coldest weather. To be sure they were apt to be sticky, if not down-right muddy; but who cared? Crossed by a network of public footpaths actual plantations extended for miles—there was more hop-ground on the north side of Farnham than there was meadow on the south side—and all these miles were free and unimpeded. Here and there, a tall quick-set hedge served to screen the precious crop from rough winds in the end of the summer; here and there a change of level separated higher and lower grounds by a few feet of all but upright bank; but no hedge or fence or ditch checked one from scampering and clambering far and wide if one wished. For no boundaries were necessary where the planted roots were never moved and space was valuable, and it would have been hard for children to do any damage to any hop-ground in the winter months. No one needed to be warned off newly dug ground—it was so rough and soft; in due season the hop-poles, even before they were festooned with the new growth, kept one to the narrow paths; but there were no other restrictions. And there can rarely have been so safe a play-ground. After picking, until women came to "strip" the bines, the poles lay in heaps, just where the pickers had piled them out of the way. Then the poles were stood up in aisles; the bines were gathered together into brown ricks for pig litter (or perhaps for bonfires for squib-night); everywhere the to-and-fro of work-folk, after the picking itself with its harum-scarum trampling was over, had worn the soft ground smooth and almost shiny; and all this could be used as a safe and happy play-ground. No officious fore-man shouted to order one off; all day long for weeks and weeks, the miles lay open for games; horses and carts (too heavy) were rarely seen in a hop-ground; none came near but good-tempered working-folk. And as this was in the winter, wintry scenes are what I recall now. No doubt there was sunshine; but in my memory the hop-grounds spread out under leaden skies. A cold and clammy wind often felt bleak; the smooth-trodden ground (with mud-water in it sometimes) reflected stormy evening tints: were those already street lights in the town? The dark was coming; it would soon be tea-time. With that prospect, so cosy and so sure, the winter dusk was delightful. There, see, a hop-pole still stood up in the ground. It added to the dishevelled look of the place; a belated rook flapping to perch atop of it made it look almost uncanny, or there was a touch of desolation in its way of holding up a battered kettle or tin pail against the sunset. Yes, that very pole would be a good one to climb!.

So the climb was attempted, in carelessness of knicker-bockers hardly meant for swarming up hop-poles. Hands and thighs were meant for that, evidently! And presently, though night was near, home was near too; and all the warmer and hungrier for one's climb, one could scamper home to tea, nice and dirty and hot, hands still tingling from the clutch of the pole.

II

Home-made toys we had. I have a dim recollection of Mary Champion (the servant at my grandfather's, and a true "sport") making kites for us in my grandfather's woodhouse. At least I remember her spreading out laths on the woodhouse floor for a kite taller than myself, and covering the laths (but how?) with old newspapers. She knotted many short folds of paper into a "tail"; made three newspaper tassels, one for the tail and one each for the shoulders; and—and there my memory can go no farther. The kite was presumably flown in the park or the hop-ground. But that cannot have been by me. I was not big enough. It must have been about this time that I saw my brother leaning his elbow on a side-board out of my reach and thought what a tall boy he was! How I admired him! Indeed he was eight and I was only four.

At this period, probably at Snasnidge ("Snailslynch") it was a pleasure to get a switch of withy and peel away many narrow rings of its thick rind—every ring about as big as the band on a cigar. Even then I thought the result unlovely, though I couldn't see why—would hardly own, even to myself, that the green unbroken rind looked lovelier before the barbarism of art had removed any of it from the slimy whiteness of the uncovered wood. Who cared? I never hesitated to peel my wand, and when I read in the Bible about Jacob (was it Jacob?) and the ring-straked cattle and the wands by the river bank, I was able to place it all at Snasnidge, having so often peeled wands there myself.

Only, in this connection, one thing puzzles me. Where can I have got the knife for ring-straking the withy? My first clasp knife—an adorable pocket knife with smooth dark brown handle—had been carefully taken by my father to be ground on the big grindstone at his shop; and when it came back anybody could indeed see, yards away, its thick edge. There was no danger of cutting my fingers. Still, I owned a knife. Proudly I showed the new tool to an uncle. He opened the knife to feel the edge, pulled the blade as far open as he could, and, affecting efforts to open it still farther, asked blandly "Will it go back?" And when I boastfully shouted "No!"—behold him pretending to pocket the knife as if I had said it wouldn't come "back" to me! But I was ready for the next uncle (there were seven of them) and kept my knife. But it was useless for cutting; my father had but too effectively saved my fingers. And now I am wondering—can it have been want of any edge to the knife that prevented me from ever making a whistle? My father would cut withy whistles for me, but I don't remember trying to make one for myself, and I can't tell how it was done. With later knives I practised a strange game, calling my knife a "toad-stabber," as I dropped it point downwards into the ground. Of any of those wonderful knives owned by some of my little comrades I was never the proud possessor; but, to be sure, having no real horse I had no need to hook stones out of horsehoofs. Still, it would have been nice to have in one's pocket a knife with a shiny hook especially designed for that purpose. These knives had each a corkscrew too (by the way, I had an uncle who amused me by saying "Querk" for cork) but I think I never used such a thing even for an ink-bottle or a little brittle, glass bottle of gum. Anyhow, a single-bladed clasp knife had to do all I wanted—sharpen slate-pencils, cut string, and all. But I don't know how I managed to cut a stick.

One other delight anyhow, came chiefly from Snasnidge —the delight of withy wands fit for bows and arrows. And there was never any doubt about the bow. Years afterwards I had a bought one made of lance-wood—a perfectly straight stick, which at last snapped after I had sent up an arrow from it out of sight into the sky. But the home-made withy bow was never straight; it deserved its name. As for the little home-made arrows—I dare say they were hazel twigs, middling straight, and cut and notched with my knife. An arrow had to do without being feathered; and any old bit of string would string the bow, if there were no knots in it.

Fishing perhaps needed a little more apparatus, and a good deal more patience, than I could command; and I did not really enjoy grubbing in the yard for worms. Still, now and again I caught and brought home in a glass bottle some miserable minnow or stickleback. A wooden bucket —if not a large wooden tub—would then be filled with the best of cool well water fresh pumped; a stone or two, a crock or two, would be dropped in to make a comfortably uneven floor and there—Why would the wretched stickleback never live? Ah—why rather did it linger so long? The laceration of its mouth by the hook was probably the least of the horrors. Cold and motionless well water replaced the limpid freedom of the running water; and the company of other fishes, and all the homeliness of a well known environment, had been lost. What knowledge the fish had was no longer of any use to it; it might as well have been blinded. In vain I dropped worms into the water. No longer served by its own senses, the lonely captive swam round and round, turned whitish; and at last, after hours, died. And I never dreamt that the whole enterprise on my part was sheer cruelty from beginning to end. I was cruel to flies—used to make little cages— barring them, as if they were wild beasts, behind pins pushed for bars through a carved-out bottle-cork. But intentional cruelty horrified me if I had eyes to see it.

Lately the odour of Friar's Balsam steaming in a bronchitis kettle brought back (for it was so strikingly real) the pleasant smell that was associated, in those far-off days, with a certain kind of wood used for carved animals. One of these, indeed—a lion four inches long or so—had a hot-looking vermilion mouth, but for the most part they were left (smelling divinely of mountain forests) clean and whitish from Swiss or Norwegian chiselling; and it is not impossible that some suggestion of village craft came to me from them. Besides the lion I had, at various times, a dog or two, a cow or two (but the ears or horns were but pegs that soon came away from the cow's head). There were horses also; and notably there was one splendid cart-horse of my brother's some eight inches long—a thing of great beauty; so smooth and clean-limbed, so well rounded, so shapely. Of other toys Jack in the Box was amusing; there was a Zoetrope; a solitaire board; there were little spiral turnings of india-rubber, furnished with snake heads and pushed into tiny wooden boxes made especially for them. These snakes—scarce three inches long—broke asunder if handled carelessly. Pop-guns could be bought; with a few inches of clock-spring steel one could make a pistol that would shoot lucifer matches; darts that would stick into a door could be made, if one had a wooden pen-holder and a pin and a bit of note-paper for sails. As for the "monkey up a stick" bought at the Fair—I never made such a thing; but to see that monkey go shooting up and down his stick—oh, the memory of it made me laugh again a few years ago, when I saw a fellow-townsman (he has gone away now) with just such a face. It lent itself—the monkey up a stick did—to cheap caricature.

"Conquerors" (shortened into "Conkers") or "Mounters" were horse-chestnuts, threaded on stout string. A gimlet bored a raw-smelling hole, and many chestnuts—

a rope or necklace of them—could be threaded on to one
string like birds' eggs. But you wanted a good strong one
for "Conquerors." Two played at that game; and indeed
you took your "Conquerors" to school with you, so as to
be ready for a challenge. Each player in his turn held up
his "conqueror"—chestnut—threaded on a string and
kept by a sufficient knot from swinging off, while his
opponent swung his own "Conqueror" against it—once
only in each turn—as hard as he could, in the hope of
breaking the other. The end of the game was when one of
the chestnuts split. A "mounter" was only a conqueror
whirled round and round and at last sent mounting up
into the sky. I don't know that there was anything in this
game except the pleasure of seeing the thing go up, with
its trailing string; yet the horse-chestnut tree often went
by the name "mounter" tree, at the season when one was
raking with one's feet over all the white and green debris
to find, if possible, one more chestnut for one's long string
at home. Chestnuts were so beautiful, until the gloss
went off.

CHAPTER XVII

WITH MY FATHER

ONE winter evening—it was already dark—I went out (no doubt my father had called us all) into the backyard to look up at the sky and see it glowing a sombre blood-red colour. When can that have been? The date could doubtless be found if it were worth while; for this spectacle was some exceptional aurora—a word I heard for the first time that night. A year or two later if not more I saw a comet in much the same way; but I had previously seen a picture of a brilliant comet curving half across the sky; and this—a poor little dim thing that might easily have been missed altogether—was not memorable as the aurora had been, but disappointing.

In such ways as this, and all unawares, I began to be a more and more interesting companion for my father. When he first took me to his brother Richard's at Frensham I don't know at all. Uncle Richard was always a favourite —always genial and happy in talk. It was good when he arrived on a Sunday morning tall and brisk stepping in his best black coat; for we all liked him, apart from the excitement I enjoyed of climbing on to his knees and feeling in his waistcoat pocket for the "peppermints" sure to be found there. Nice little white peppermints these were, about as big as a shilling. The brimstone yellow ones my grandmother (my mother's mother) used to pop into my mouth in church were, to be sure, a trifle larger, and worth having—in church; but they were not really so delectable as Uncle Richard's white ones. West Surrey crackled pleasantly in his voice—there was a slight resonance; the *r*'s sounded strong, and there was no uncertainty about the *a*'s and *e*'s. I didn't know or care then that he was a very active and able wheelwright; but I know now that a good craftsman does unfold that quick, confident, good-tempered manner Uncle Richard had. Of course it was to see his father that he so often walked over from Frensham on Sunday mornings; but he and my father had a venture together in hops, and plenty of other local interests; while I, for my part, was never once disappointed of peppermints.

For a change, it was a happy treat sometimes to wander over to Frensham with my father, to see Uncle Richard. I say "wander," because no doubt the expedition took a long time. Why should it not? There was no hurry. There were no motor-cars then to destroy the Sunday morning quiet; no villas to ruin the heaths. My father could go dreaming quietly forward along the empty road and we children could clamber and scramble near him, into the ditches and up the roadside banks. (He had been wont in earlier years, I learnt afterwards, to roam over that track with his sister Margaret, botanising—they two kindling one another's interest, though there were few books or teachers for them.) Was there any wild thyme? I do not remember any; yet clear woody scents from heath and brake fern were plentiful before the road was tarred and while the whole upland lay unfenced on the slopes. And of course it was sunny. It had to be nice summer weather, or we should not have started. The road was solitary, but always alive and full of light.

One thing stands out clearly enough in my memory, and puzzlingly too. What day of the week can it have been, when my father was free to take me to Frensham, though another man was free to be at work in the Bourne? To be sure, it has never been an unknown thing for a Bourne man to be gardening on a Sunday morning; but this man was not gardening. He was cleaving laths; and the man I think he must have been would certainly not have broken the fourth commandment. Son of a certain tall tailor in Farnham, whom my father once pointed out as being able to repeat Paradise Lost all through (a thing that impressed me very little), this lath-cleaver was himself of such piety that he would have dreaded to break the Sabbath, but might have gloried in hurting Church of England feelings by disregarding any other church festival. But which? Christmas was out of the question; Good Friday could hardly have been other than too early in the year; and Bank Holidays I think had not been invented, or at any rate observed, by then. I can only guess that this was Whitsun Monday or some special public holiday near Midsummer, that being the best if not the only season for cleaving oak. Anyhow, in the summer, near the present Post Office in the Bourne, my attention was drawn to a man cleaving laths. This much at least I am sure of. As we stood to watch, of course to my father, acquainted with the man and himself a connoisseur of timber work, the whole operation would be fascinating. He probably knew the woods the oak came from, understood the man's movements and appreciated his tools, felt uplifted at the scent of the oak sap and at the familiar splitting sound; and in fact tasted the craftsman's never-failing delight, beyond the reach of any words, when things themselves talk their own special talk. I, for my part, could only look on without much interest, to tell the truth. Yet there is little doubt that the sight gave value to the whole of that day; for I have a dim recollection that it had to be spoken of to Uncle Richard.

Did I have any peppermints then? I do not know, but it is likely enough. It is likely enough too, though that also I do not know now, that I picked strawberries, for there was a strawberry-bed in my uncle's garden. Everywhere was the comfort of clear space, so much better than our cramped yard at home. Across the road was a wheelwright's shop and a smithy; and seen between the apple-trees and down the flower-bordered paths and beyond the village and the tree-filled river valley, the slopes of Hindhead lifted silently to a level skyline miles away.

Yes, there was plenty of room in that rustic garden— room to tear about and get hot, from well to thatched summer-house. The summer-house itself was a treat, though older people did find it infested with earwigs or buzzing flies. To me it seemed, with its thatch and hard wooden seats, like the very heart of the country—pleasant and sure as Uncle Richard himself. We doubtless had plenty of nice things to eat at Millbridge—for there was the village provision shop at my uncle's, besides a bake-house.

I think it was an evening, when my father took me to the big chalk-pit below the fence at Farnham park. The chalk-pit was almost literally "below"; for the chalk had been quarried-in so close that for a few yards the sills of the fence had been built out on special beams over the edge of the pit. A nasty dangerous place it looked. Choking smoke, drifting into the park from the lime-kiln across the pit, sometimes drove one away from that neighbourhood altogether. A break in the endless green hop-ground, the white chalk-pit lay uninviting, and I had never been into it. But that summer evening, in my father's company, all was different. No men at work there would order one off; it would be safe to go and peer over into the empty lime-kiln; to follow that mysterious track of white ruts winding up from the street through the hops —well, it was worth while to go anywhere with my father. Had he any business-call there? Some broken-down cart or wheel to report upon? Whatever his errand may have been he took me with him; and when at last we got into the chalk-pit—wonders will never cease!—he picked up a knob of chalk about as big as his fist, and breaking it, showed me a little crinkled shell, steel blue, embedded in the white chalk! It was the first "fossil" I ever saw, and he may have told me much about it; but he left unexplained how he knew it was there, as I was sure he did. That remained a mystery about fossils for a long time. How did anyone know the right stone to break?

With my father's help I learnt to look in his Anne Pratt for the names of the ferns we found and of other plants he seemed interested in; and by and by he took me on other business expeditions with him, as soon as I was man enough for the longer walks involved. Indeed, twice we had a conveyance. It was in a little basketwork pony-

phaeton (Stokes of West Street was the owner of it, a few
Farnham folk may like to recall) that we went to Well to
buy some trees at Collier's there; and I think it was in a
wagonette (Uncle Richard going too) that we drove past
Headley and "The Shant," and saw ash-butts lying in
steep hollows, and I heard of the difficulty of hauling
timber out of bad places. But for the nearer outings we
walked.

For instance, we walked, as I have already told, into the
"Pleasure Grounds" in Farnham Park on some business
with the Keeper; and I can recall further expeditions—to
a certain park at Seale amongst others, where I seem to
have tasted a very pleasing air of country-house affluence
and ease in a steward's room and in a sleepy and well-
groomed courtyard. But I was probably a little older then.
No doubt my father was buying timber, as no doubt also
he was at an earlier time when I was at Tilford with him.
He had probably been measuring trees. For he had with
him a timber-measuring tape which I was allowed to help
hold up when, for curiosity, he measured the circumference
of "The King's Oak" on Tilford Green. At four feet or
so from the ground the famous tree was found to measure
twenty-three and a half feet round, somewhere about the
year 1870.

And with this companionship my world grew picturesque
if not romantic. From the top of Castle Steps could be
seen across Farnham valley the level line of the opposite
hill stretching towards the Holt forest three miles away
This ridge was fringed, towards Shortheath especially,
with hedgerow trees which seemed to be watching the

weather; and one of these trees my father indicated to me, saying it was a sentinel! Exact! It happened that I had had a drawing copy at school, showing a soldier on horseback at nightfall gazing out into rainy weather. And there on the horizon, this tree seemed to be steadfastly gazing. Its slanting branches took the storm wind just like the soldier's wind-swept cloak. It faced towards a strange country. At nightfall, in the winter, clouds and the forest added loneliness to it. It was on the watch! By calling it "The Sentinel" my father interpreted and endeared to me all that stretch of Surrey landscape.

CHAPTER XV

CANON HOSTE, AND OTHER CHURCHMEN

THE tale of the difference between Bishop Sumner and Mr John Andrews the butcher has been published, and need not be told here; it is curious, though, that certain details relating to the same tale should find a place in my own recollections. Sundry of these recollections do however make it real to me and do belong to my childhood, dim though the earliest of them are.

In the first place, I did actually see Mr Andrews in the flesh. At some time I went to his shop, where "Old Johnny" or "Old Jacky" as they sometimes called him, was sitting by a fire in a room behind the shop. As he always has had the reputation of being no less kind (if facetious) to little children than he was sympathetic to "The Poor," and as I do not remember disliking the errand, I take it for granted that my little shopping expedition went off comfortably, and that Mr Andrews was really the benignant clean-shaved largish lounging man I have always thought him—comical perhaps, but the reverse of churlish. A very rich man, it amused him to speak his mind to the Bishop. I must have been familiar with the sight of him, though his shop was round the corner of Castle Street, quite out of my way. An odd thing (but this likewise is very dim) is that I seem to have seen the little throng of poor folk outside his shop on a Sunday morning, waiting to buy the joints it pleased him to sell very cheap at such times.

This also is odd: Bishop Sumner—like "Old Johnny" —was a familiar figure to my eyes. His silvery gray hair— the subject of admiring remark throughout Farnham— practically labelled him as he leant back in his carriage on his way to church, driving past Mr Andrews's shop with its collection of out-at-elbows folk. Did someone take me to see the scene of Mr Andrews's flouting of the great man? One other carriage used to drive to church; but the owner inside it was after all only a local gentleman, not Lord of the Manor; and we did but smile to see the row of domestic servants being taken to church atop of this gentleman's carriage—they looked so proper, and one thought with so little respect of the big-wig within shielded from disagreeable weather. On the other hand one had to respect my Lord Bishop; who may have left his servants behind in the Castle, yet could not drive to church without two flunkeys clinging to the back of his carriage. Yes verily! he was a grandee and no mistake! But did I see those flunkeys myself? If not, why do the two men in the mental picture I form of that weekly display wear tight yellow stockings? Old Johnny is said to have seen them and re- sented them; even to have returned a defiant answer to the Bishop, the Bishop having sent a protest against being obliged to pass a shop open for poor folk, when on his way to church on a Sunday morning. Amongst other reasons for supposing that Farnham folk were a good deal interested, one is that I should have any memory at all of this scene, which could hardly have come before my eyes unless somebody had taken me to see.

Yet if people chuckled with Mr Andrews, and secretly

formed thoughts of their own about church-going and servants and so on, still the Bishop was far and away the most important person in the neighbourhood. The name "bishop's holding" given to the many copyhold tenures throughout the manor of Farnham indicates the size of the holding. So when at last he died in the Castle, the town seems to have bated its breath. On the day of the funeral the shops were shut, and—just at one tiny patch here my memory grows vivid. It sees me, not alone but with a sister or two, at East Street in the loft over the wheel-wright's shop, which presumably had ceased work; and we were staring out of the window to see the funeral procession go by. For Bishop Sumner was buried at Hale Church—I don't know why—and tradesmen of any self-respect followed the coffin. I watched them going slowly two by two along East Street. Was Mr Andrews one of them? Likely enough. There were many I recognised then, in that long procession of black-coated undrilled men. But I only remember now seeing my father go by with the rest.

At "the Bishop's Sale," or on one of the days before, I was able for the first and only time to get to the top of the Castle. From a bedroom there or from the leads in front of it, I saw a wide view, with Hindhead, so smooth-ridged (for as yet there was no building there) lying right across the south. A bit of carving near that bedroom fireplace took my eye. What it was I clean forget—the point is that then (for perhaps the first time in my life) something seized my attention as a thing to look at for its very charm and antiquity.

Of the sale itself I did but hear, and my only recollection is that the old ale, said to be out-of-the-way strong, was sold at a great price. Seeing how many years afterwards "Bishop's Ale" was still purchaseable in Farnham, there must have been huge quantities of it. A tale went round that the Castle brewhouse-men had once made difficulties about the long way it was to carry it down into the cellars, but had yielded at his lordship's retorting that they were always willing enough to carry it up!

Of more importance than the Bishop of Winchester to my childish eyes was the Archdeacon of Surrey, resident then in Farnham as rector. Archdeacons of Surrey had often been, *ex officio*, Rectors of Farnham. Of Archdeacon Utterton I remember chiefly the clerical gaiters, they being at the right height for a child to notice. Otherwise I remember only that he annoyed my mother once by stopping a newspaper boy and trying to buy a paper, though the boy was only delivering papers to regular customers and had none to sell.

What happened to the Archdeacon? A new Bishop (Wilberforce had never come into residence; and it was Harold Browne now) was at the Castle; and by and by he appointed a new Rector of Farnham. The Archdeacon had lived sumptuously in Castle Street; but for Mr Hoste— a tall man, with a big family—the Rectory (a more obscure place) was done-up, while the ancient Vicarage across the churchyard was made ready for a relative of his.

And soon I heard for the first time in my life of church disputes. For Mr Hoste began by giving offence. His face looked kindly—if a child could look up so far; and he seemed all right when I saw him walking along the pavement past our shop. Moreover I heard him "read himself in" at the Parish Church; and through all the Thirty-nine Articles there was nothing to dislike in his steady level voice. (Long afterwards I realised that it was sheer pleasure to hear him read.) And yet, ere long it grew all too plain that people were feeling affronted!

What was wrong? Perhaps he was a trifle "High," it was hinted. Or possibly the introduction into Farnham of the "Hymns Ancient and Modern" may have been an unnecessary expense due to him. But the serious thing—somehow I hadn't noticed it, yet what cause for dismay!—was that he preached in a white surplice instead of in a black gown! At that, various citizens marked their displeasure by going elsewhere—a little ostentatiously perhaps. One became a pillar of Wrecclesham Church; while my father, as told already, chose to go to Hale. Very punctilious he was, too, in his attendances. I don't think there were any more Sunday morning walks to Frensham. My father had to testify against preaching in a white surplice, and he testified every week.

Did he really care? Or was it not rather just perversity? We children often walked to Hale Church with him; where Mr Rowe preached in black, I suppose, though I do not know that he did. At Hale Church I saw various queer things—amongst them one or two odd-looking men whom their grand-children in Farnham at this day might be willing to forget. Also there was a sexton, grim-faced, who prowled about with a cane to keep the boys in order. I liked the walk to Hale Church, along the lower side of

Farnham Park. Yet I often went to Farnham Parish
Church—on Sunday evenings instead of afternoons as I
grew older. And very good it was. I think I have never
elsewhere known such tranquillity as I felt then in that
quiet church on still summer evenings, listening to the
swifts screaming round and round outside, and uplifted
all the time by Mr Hoste's perfectly managed voice
within. From him the cadences of Evensong fell rich and
soothing, as if the ripeness and value they had gained in
the centuries were being unlocked again for one's special
behoof. Somehow his composure, echoing from the candle-
lit chancel, expressed the emotion of long generations,
which was renewed in one's-self, so that man's life seemed
dignified by the touch of past ages. Of course other things
helped to kindle that feeling—the ample cool aisles, the
colours and the curves and the woodwork, the stealing on
of evening shadows, the sense of old-world associations—
but there is no doubt that it all took richer meaning from
the stately English sentences, well-known and familiar,
ringing so quiet and even through the listening church.
Mr Hoste himself must have felt it, and with enthusiasm,
though I am not persuaded that he knew by what me-
chanism—of colours and curves and voice tones and
associations—the effect was produced. Perhaps he did not
know. His sermons too often seemed foolishness even to
me, though possibly memory plays me false.

Can I really have heard him tell how all who dissented
from the Church of England were doomed to perdition?
or that when the wind blew open the church door Satan
was at work? I once watched the south door quietly

swinging ajar, but nothing happened that seemed to me unpleasant. But I probably misunderstood; and anyhow one's mind easily forgets rubbishy opinions, while one's tissues take permanent growth from feelings. Taste grows without thought and perhaps I owe some taste for serenity to Canon Hoste. He became honorary canon of Winchester; and by the time he left, worn out, for a lighter cure, and died of cancer in the throat, the very dissenters had learnt to revere him as a kindlier man—a more true-hearted man—than most, and of matchless veracity.

CHAPTER XIX

AUTUMN MANŒUVRES

I FIND it not quite easy—in fact I am not able at all—to separate from my many memories connected with Aldershot Camp the few things that ought to be amongst these reminiscences of childhood. Of course there is the general atmosphere of Aldershot—not exactly a pleasant atmosphere in those far-off days. Farnham did not at all like Aldershot or its people. We regarded the town as an upstart place that had sprung within living memory from nothing but a most mean village. And we never thought it inconsistent with our own good manners to behave superciliously to Aldershot people, as if the sharp practice of some of them was to be expected of them all. At school it was a handicap to a boy's popularity to have come from Aldershot.

As I had never seen any of the country places near the Camp, so too it never occurred to me ever to surmise how the whole neighbourhood was being demoralised; how servant-girls were more flighty and labouring folk less to be trusted than of old, with soldiers and soldiering-life so close at hand. I did not dream that in the very look of lane and heath, of field and park and meadow, where gas-works and asphalt paths and town litter were encroaching, country beauty was giving place to meanness, sordidness, squalor. Perhaps I did realise that if a young man was said to have "gone for a soldier" it was as bad as saying he had gone to the Devil, and that Farnham would never hear of him again. And even though we need not have been quite

so pharisaical, it is true that ugly sides of soldiering were
only too plainly to be seen and heard. Soldiers were often
drunken and rowdy in Farnham streets; even officers
could not always command respect amongst us. To be
sure, some of the leading residents of Farnham—a colonel
or two, perhaps a general—left nothing to be desired.
These residents lived in the right houses, took the lead
even of the leading gentry, and were in short beyond
criticism. But whether all officers were quite on the level
of gentlemen was not so sure. Some of them swore a good
deal; kept dogs—ladies, perhaps; played cards; smoked
cigars. Did they always pay their bills? Were they in-
clined to be a bit raffish? Was there sometimes, in regard
to them, a disapproval which even a child could feel, in
slow-going old Farnham?

There was no disapproval, or at least in later years there
was none, of the excitement that military marching music
often raised in our street; when soldiers were tramping
through. Brass bands were comparatively common. Sometimes bagpipes, followed by stalwart bare-kneed men,
would set one's blood dancing; sometimes even a "mounted
band," with trumpets and kettle-drums, went prancing
proudly before cavalry. And did not band-masters go
grandly, swinging huge ornate sticks? and swanking
drummers, bending back behind leopard-skins and big
drums, toss their drum-sticks cleverly into the air, to catch
them again exactly and at the right moment for another
bang? or bugle-men swing their bugles to their lips with
an air when the fifes and drums made pause for their
gallant call? And was it not good to watch the Highland

kilts all along the street swinging rhythmically this way and then that? and the swaying feathers of the Highland head-gear? or perhaps to see some sacred mascot—some goat or antelope or dog pattering along in front of a whole regiment? Thousands of men, smoking, singing, sweating and dusty on hot summer days and wearing green branches to cool their heated faces; or hundreds of baggage wag-gons; or endless streams of guns; or of spare horses; or stray officers on horseback tearing to and fro along the lines of marching men and looking plagued; or little bevies of gilt-spurred superior officers looking important before their grooms. These items—in endless variety—enlivened Farnham week after week for years (in fact until The War altered everything); but while I remember how the marching men watched the upstairs windows to greet maid-servants, and how workmen stopped work, while traffic was blocked, and the side-walks grew crowded, be-cause soldiers were passing, and schools emptied and children shouted "Any more?" after the last men in sight —while these things are fresh enough in my memory—I cannot say for certain whether as a little boy I did or did not grow familiar with any of them. The one thing I do remember was something quite different—something seen that once only and unlike anything before or since—namely, the passing of some of the equipment through Farnham for the first Autumn Manœuvres.

At four in the morning, or as soon after as there was daylight enough for getting dressed[1], I stood on the pave-

---

[1] Of course in those days, long before "summer time" had been thought of, dawn was near at hand at four in the morning.

ment in front of our little shop, watching the strange procession. I cannot have been alone there though I have no memory of others; but sleep in Farnham would have been out of the question with that rattle going through; and I surmise that many Farnhamites besides myself had turned out of bed and into the street, with rough hair and in slippers, to watch what was going by in the grey of the morning.

For, as aforesaid, it was a strange procession. It must have been still dark when the Camp was left, for these things would not hurry all those miles. Farm horses with loaded waggons behind them will not gallop far in any case, and in this case some sort of order, if not time, had to be kept. At any rate, that is what the procession consisted of —farm horses with farm waggons; or commercial van and dray horses, with their vans and drays. For either there was no Army Service Corps then; or (more likely) what there was was insufficient for these unprecedented manœuvres, and the whole neighbourhood was being drawn upon. Many of the vehicles must have been known to my father if, as is likely, he also was watching the procession; but, for my part, I only stared—and wondered.

Did I hear remarks too? Or what is it has kept in my mind, all these years, a feeling that spectators were commenting on some of those waggon loads as upon improprieties? What can have preserved even a memory of odd things witnessed? Odd things indeed! Not only was there load after load of equipment for the rank and file. I noted also in the hired waggons besides tents and much necessary baggage, pianos, wicker easy chairs, circular baths, piled up in great profusion—I remember these things, and remember wondering why officers could not do without them even when travelling.

Now, after half a century and more, I have learnt not to be surprised at such things; on the other hand, I wonder now, as I did not then, how that vast procession was got on the road at all. Soon after four it was passing through Farnham Street, at least three miles from any possible starting place; and it was still rumbling away westwards when I went back to bed again about six o'clock. At that hour my father presumably went off (as he always did) to his work in East Street; at any rate, about six o'clock I went back to bed again—though the show was not over— feeling a little proud of myself for having got up at four like a man! I fancy I felt sleepy too; as well a child might, after gaping for two hours at things moving past; at vans and waggons, at strange loads, at unaccustomed horses and men, lumbering along in endless stream. One after the other still they kept coming round the far bend of the street. But if I had not seen it, I should not believe it now. The thing was impossible. I know I saw the procession go by; yet how can it have been assembled and the waggons packed and arranged and started in order? How can it have got as far as Farnham with men and horses unused to discipline and, probably, absurd ill-mannered easy-chair young officers making mere loud-voiced confusion? One would say it could not have been done. It was incredible, in much the same way as our muddling through "The Great War" is incredible to-day. Yet, I saw it done. And if many were incompetent, there must have been some-

where at Aldershot one organiser supremely capable of
his job, to get the first Autumn Manœuvres started on
the road.

A piece of sheer slackness was the cause of one other
excitement from Aldershot Camp I witnessed at about
the same time. Here once more my memory may be con-
fused with more recent ones; for I do not really know that
this first stampede (that was a new word I picked up then)
led many horses to horrible disaster. In after years two or
three affairs of the sort ended in horses being found so
injured that they had to be shot; and this probably happened in the case in question. If, however, I heard of it
at the time, I have forgotten it now. What I do recall is,
sudden little groups—a dozen at a time perhaps (they may
have numbered two or three hundred in all)—of riderless
horses, unharnessed, tearing in wild panic through Farnham town. It was a cloudy summer evening, the street
was very quiet; I stood in the little shop while my mother
behind the counter was serving a certain tradesman whose
name may as well be forgotten. He, holding the glass
door ajar, peeped out into the street. Then suddenly,
from East Street, arose another thundering of hoofs, the
tradesman slammed the door, and through the glass I saw
another rush of horses tearing by like mad between the
dingy old houses.

Unfortunately for the tradesman (how scornfully my
mother spoke of him afterwards!) shutting our shop door
so that he himself might feel the safer he shut it in the face
of my mother's own mother! For my grandmother (with
a sister of mine, I am told) had just arrived back from

Frensham. She was even then coming in at the shop door, escaping from real peril out there on the pavement, when the timid tradesman shut her out. He cannot have seen the Frensham pony-chaise drawn up by the curb! Indeed, I do not seem to have seen it very accurately myself; for my own memory pictures not a basket chaise but a market cart from Farnborough; and in that picture there is no hurrying woman and little girl; hardly even a scared gentleman shutting them out of safety. All I see is a narrow old street partly blocked by a conveyance standing at one side of it, and frightened horses tearing by towards West Street at night-fall. What had happened? It was told afterwards (and I heard as much as I desired to know) that a number of horses at Aldershot (artillery horses I think) had slipped their picket (or some such phrase) and finding themselves free had galloped away, becoming more and more terrified by their own loud-hoofed and clattering impetuosity, and with only herd-panic instead of the guidance they were used to.

CHAPTER XX

MR POPPLETON'S

I DON'T know why I left Miss May's; probably I was thought too big for that mixed school. It is as a very small boy that I see myself at Mr Poppleton's, a few doors nearer my home. Very small, but complacent, plump, and well pleased to be promoted to this "boys' school." In that hazy vision of many years ago, my brother and two or three others as big as himself are looking down at me amused and good-tempered. I fancy that they then and there found a nickname for me—"Farmer" (it was not destined to stick)—and I suspect now, though I didn't dream of such a thing at the time, that my brother was making things go smoothly for me. To be sure everybody at that school treated me indulgently, almost as if I was a darling. And it always was so afterwards. No schoolmaster, for instance, ever gave me a tanning. Mr Poppleton himself (I don't remember that he used a cane on anyone) had a pleasant trick of digging boys in the back with his thumb stiffened out in front of clenched knuckles; and this must have been very unpleasant, to judge from the helpless shrinkings and writhings and blubberings of other little boys sitting beside me, not knowing when they would be assaulted. (One, I remember, often victimised, whimpered to me one day that he wished the affliction would "break his belt." That was his constant hope. A broken belt would perhaps bring about interference and protection from a father, indifferent to mere backs.) But

I myself was never thumped or touched in any way. My worst trouble (save for once) was being "kept in," my lesson being "returned"—either unlearnt or ill-prepared. This happening to me one afternoon, when I might otherwise have been running home to tea, the shocking disaster broke me down and I wept copiously; though a little boy beside me—Dick by name—compassionately assured me that being "kept in" didn't matter. He indeed was used to it, I knew, and was far from tears.

Presumably I learnt something worth while at Poppleton's but it would be easy to make too much of it. It was there I was shown how to "do" a long division "sum," sprawling it across my slate from the left-hand corner at the top towards the right-hand corner at the bottom, with a "remainder" looking like a pretty tail. "Rule of three" I learnt too, discovering why it was called that; and at last I found my way into vulgar fractions; even into decimals, with "repeaters." "Practice" no doubt was unfolded to me; "money sums" too; but none of these introductions has left the slightest trace on my memory. One detail I re-discover rather by inference. I must have begun algebra. For at my next school I had to have a new text-book, Todhunter's I think; my own being discarded, not because it was a bad book, but because its author, Colenso, was a wicked man. Had I not been so taught I might not have known of scepticism for years! Now that I think of algebra, a dim feeling of delight in the cuteness of simple equations comes back to me, with a supposition that some of this must have been due to Mr Poppleton's instructions. In something the same way I know I started Latin. Not that I remember any actual start; but a boy in the class with me rendered "*amo te indies*" as "I love the Indian," which I knew to be a bad guess. I learnt the declensions in an order (Nominative, Genitive, Dative, and so on) not accepted afterwards at the Grammar School. I began French with Ahn's (or was it Allman's) *First French Course*; and Grammar with a little book whose name I have forgotten. The interest I found later (at the Grammar School) in Morell's *Grammar and Analysis* must have been kindled by Mr Poppleton when he started me on to that book.

Indeed, the more I think of "Old Pop" the more. I respect him. It's true he was very conceited (perhaps he had one good pupil in that) but the letters "L.C.P." after his name (he also added F.S.E., F.S.A.) meant more merit in him than Farnham guessed, when L.C.P. was amplified into "Lazy Conceited Puppydog." There are men living in Farnham to-day who are a credit to him—I doubt if the Grammar School turned out any better; and Mr Poppleton had none of the advantages of the rival school. There must have been five-and-twenty or thirty boys under him in my time; and he managed their schooling all himself, or with next to no assistance. One very inefficient usher there was once—doubtless a lonely fellow—who "acted the goat" to the applause of some of the bigger boys; and at one time old Mrs Poppleton ("Lovey Dovey" her husband used to call her) helped with a class of little boys. Perhaps she was a kind old woman—I seem to see a silly and conceited smile behind spectacles when I think of her—and she had her hands full with the house-work (for I think there was no servant of any sort) but little boys can rarely have had a more futile teacher. She, or the usher in his time, occupied a little low desk near the fire-place. Mr Poppleton himself, behind a table, sat on a platform against the wall facing the fire-place. There, he had the whole school under his eye. One big square room, in fact—that was all it was. There was no class-room or lobby. Double doors, the upper half panelled in glass, opened directly upon two steps down into the little play-ground, which sloped still farther down towards the dwelling-house and the passage into East Street. Perhaps Mr Poppleton could see down into the play-ground, as well as over all the schoolroom.

There, if you returned up the two steps into that room from the play-ground, on the right hand was the fire-place faced by the platform against the opposite wall, as already said. But Mr Poppleton was not always, perhaps was not often, on the platform. He might be walking round behind the small boys at the desks, where it was temptingly easy to thump his thumb into them if they were tiresome, or if he himself felt cross. On either side of the glass doors as soon as you got within, on your right and also on your left a big window supplied all the light; and all along, under each window, was a desk—a sloping bench close up to the window frame—for little boys. Then, the wall being reached (room for two more boys there) the row of desks turned back, facing the other way. Whereas the first-named row, touching the windows, gave a look-out (through clear glass too) into the play-ground, the other row on the contrary faced towards the middle of the room. Thus there were two rows of boys; one row facing the play-ground; the other, divided from it by a gangway, sitting with their backs to the first. So these latter could see the fire and the platform, and all the rest of the room. Certainly in the summer the front benches facing the sunny window were more cheerful than the others. They were shaded too (at least partially) by an apple tree in the play-ground. (Come to think of it, I never saw apples there, or even blossom; but I have never doubted that it was an apple tree.) Across on the farther side of the schoolroom opposite the door, ran an exactly similar arrangement—two rows of boys, back to back, at sloping benches; and at either end of the gangway between them a short cross-bench. Of course it was darker and more dingy at the back, there being no window or glass door—nothing but the discoloured wall. (I didn't think of the hop-ground outside, sloping up towards the park.) But apart from these differences, the front of the school and the back were just alike; and between the two halves, where the platform faced the fire-place, was an open space of floor. Boys could stand in a half ring there, reading aloud, or repeating their lessons, to Mr Poppleton on the platform. I was standing there when I heard about "I love the Indian."

To the best of my belief the walls were bare. At home a thin atlas with uncoloured maps was amongst my books and I knew its use, admiring greatly what seemed to me an immense coloured atlas my sister had at Miss Stratford's. But I saw nothing of the sort at Mr Poppleton's. Indeed, I have reason to suppose that Mr Poppleton had no value for such things. He cared rather for engineering and mathematics; and it was only because any good school had to teach history and geography that he concerned himself with those subjects. He had a simple way of teaching matters that did not interest him. Geography, for its part (like grammar), was learnt "by heart"—nine or ten lines a day, marked in one's book and repeated (as one repeated the Church Catechism) in a class, with one's hands behind one's back. Either one "knew" one's geography, or didn't know it and was "kept in" (probably to learn it, but *I* thought only for punishment). One other thing there was. Every evening *Eve's Examiner* had to be dealt with in writing for a "home lesson"; and once a week its questions were in geography. How other boys managed I do not know. To me, this examination in geography was fairly easy because on a bookshelf at home was Maunder's *Treasury of Knowledge*, containing, my brother had found (and in due time he showed me), a "New Universal Gazetteer." With that the questions in *Eve's Examiner* could usually be answered easily. In the rare event of that failing, there was always one's father; and if even he didn't know the answer *Eve's Examiner* required, it obviously was not worth knowing, and perhaps nobody knew it!

History we did not have even to memorise. It is true, in a notable contest with George Mason to settle who should be head of the school, my brother learnt "by heart" some chapters of a History of Rome[1]. But for English History a little book we used (and I don't think it was "Little Arthur's History" either) served as a class

---

[1] I held the book, to "hear" him; and I still remember one passage, something like this : "Pompey, Cicero and Caesar—these were the three men destined to control the affairs of the Roman Empire."

reading-book too. This we read out sentence by sentence (measuring by "full-stops")—one boy one sentence, as if we were reading verses in the Bible; and some of these sentences stick in my memory now[1].

For "writing" we had copy-books—"Large Hand," "Round Hand," and "Small Hand." (A full copy-book, taken home, served very well for a scrap-book, the pages being covered with illustrations cut square and stuck in anyhow so that they fitted without gaps.) In whatever hand, you filled a line and then wrote it again and again until the page was full. So, having filled one left-hand side, in large hand, with "Govern your Temper" and got into the habit of writing capital G, I began the opposite side too with Govern and wrote "Govern your Parents," instead of "Honour your Parents," in large hand. For further practice in small hand we had "Commercial Letters"—copper-plate models on blue paper pasted on card-board, with which was included one set on white paper. As these were in French I did not try to understand what they were about; but even then I admired them; and I still regret that no one showed me how to make my own writing look as nice.

Boarders there were, but I know little or nothing of

---

[1] "A man who has ungrateful and wicked children," the book said, apropos of Henry II and his rebellious sons, "never can be happy." Again, when the Duke of Gloucester told how Jane Shore was practising witchcraft against him, "Lord Hastings" began some timid speech with "If." "'If'" said the Protector, in a loud voice, "Dost thou answer me with 'If'?" and it soon led to "Off with his head!" So much for Hastings. I believe it was this book that introduced me to Alfred and the Cakes, and to the King who "never smiled again"; and gave me the names of Lambert Simnel and Perkin Warbeck, one of whom was a "scullion."

their life, or even approximately how many they numbered, most of us in the school being day-boys. The school had no bath-room; it boasted no matron or cook, or in fact any servant whatever. Mr and Mrs Poppleton must have done all the work themselves, perhaps with a little incompetent help from the boarders[1]. One room, ten foot square or so, full of books and called "The Library," no doubt served Mr Poppleton as an office. It faced the street. The rest of the house had to supply dormitory, kitchen, scullery, and living-room—none of which I ever saw, but all of which must have been the scene of toil by Mrs Poppleton, when she was not mending, or darning, or doing laundry-work, or scrubbing-out the schoolroom, or window cleaning, or any other little job like that. At all these jobs no doubt Mr Poppleton took his share, to say nothing of one other which has not yet been hinted at. Even with half a dozen boarders if no more, some supervision would be required —some evening lesson-learning and so on. Meals too would have to be presided over.

A special dodge, which I thought admirably clever, lightened the house-work in regard to meals. The room given over to the boarders—probably the only one available—was the first-floor back room. It gave a view across the play-ground to the school-room thirty yards away, and was a cheerful room enough. A narrow staircase twisted up to it (house-space being cramped in old Farnham) from the passage that came from the street; and, since it was in

---

[1] It was a boarder (an admired runner then, a substantial tradesman in another town now) who was enlisted to wring the neck of a fowl, but failed to kill the bird.

this room that the boarders had their food, there would have been a deal of carrying up and down these twisty stairs, but for Mr Poppleton's ingenious device. In a corner of the room he had fashioned a little hand-lift for food and plates and dishes or any light thing from the kitchen below. As I was fairly familiar with this wonder (though its working never ceased to be a miracle to stare at) I must occasionally have gone into this common room of the boarders; yet when can that have been?

Twice only am I sure of having gone there. I sat there at a very juvenile examination, memorable only because I felt so large and experienced beside a shy child, smaller than myself, who had come in for that occasion from Miss May's infant school. The other time was at some school festival—Mr Poppleton's birthday, perhaps—when, if it was interesting to watch the lift, it was better still to feel convivial, to be present while a few daring fellows sang songs, and in fact be in a real Party! Was it George Grove who sang that sentimental ballad about "Far far away?" "Where are now those happy faces," it said, "That I knew so long ago?" I still remember the delicious yearning sob excited by that song. It cannot but have been a successful evening, if the other boys enjoyed themselves as well as I did. I, for my part, seem to have enjoyed it so well as to have forgotten all other occasions of entering that room.

It speaks well for the school that I should have heard no whisper of complaint in so many years. The boarders, so far as I know to the contrary, were well fed and well cared for. There might have been a little more washing, perhaps, but the opportunities in all Farnham were not too many, and Mr and Mrs Poppleton had a good many things to attend to.

For some reason which I never fathomed Mr Poppleton disliked his boarders to send letters to the post unknown to him. Had he anything to conceal from the parents? It is unlikely. On Thursday, the town market day, the schools had half-holiday and farmers were wont to visit their children at school. In short, there was plenty of opportunity for boarders to complain if they wanted to. But if one of them wanted to flirt with one of the girls at Miss Stratford's? Anyhow, Mr Poppleton disapproved of his boarders posting letters—disapproved strongly, as at last I knew. I had posted a letter for a boy named Wolsey (that will do for his name, his home was a farm nine or ten miles away) and some days later I was aware of trouble in the school. Mr Poppleton was storming because Wolsey (and I liked Wolsey, and remember now how red his face looked) had been smuggling letters to the post, and some unknown day-boy must have been the carrier! This began to sound very shocking; for Mr Poppleton was quite stuffy with indignation. So by and by, to clear up an unpleasant situation, I said it was I who had posted the letter. *"You?"* Mr Poppleton seemed genuinely hurt and surprised. Yet even then he did not lay hands on me. I only had to move to the other side of the room at once, as if I was no longer to be trusted there at the back where the boarders sat. Perhaps Mr Poppleton upbraided me further—I don't know now that he did; and in the next play-time Wolsey suggested that I might as well have held my tongue. But I suffered no other punishment.

As I am not aware of any grouping into Forms or
Classes (Mr Poppleton attended personally to us all), and
as slates, copy-books, reading-books, and so on, were kept
in stacks so that no boy needed a "desk" of his own, so
I recall no part of the school-room (except the platform itself!) in which I do not seem to have sat at one time or
another, different places in it coming back to my memory
as I recall this or that incident, this or that school-fellow.
I am sitting with my back to the light as I learn from the
boy next me how to make "Tincture." (That is no part
of "book-learning." It is only for the users of slates.) In
this fascinating pursuit you scrape your slate-pencil into
the ink; and the black mud thus obtained is "Tincture."
Like other products of art, it is interesting but of no
earthly use. You have to be happily idle to get it, leaving
others to work. At another desk, beside another boy
("Zoo" we called him), I am overcome with admiring
envy of a drawing (done on paper, at his home) of an
Indian lying dead on the ground, his head on his arm.
Indians, alive or dead, seemed all that mattered. Another
time—and this was when flickering apple-leaf shadows
dappled our sunny bench against the window—a boy
turned to me, and said very gravely, "*He's* the man. Don't
you think so?" It happened that I didn't "think so." As
my father didn't believe in the "claimant," Arthur Orton's
pretence to be Roger Tichborne could not be admitted,
to oblige my wrong-headed school-fellow.

One birthday party I recall; whose, I do not know.
We met in the school-room. George Grove's song was
"As I went through my father's farm One bright May

morning early"—an interminable piece, which we all thought delightfully comic as the different things in a farm-yard were mentioned. Was there not some realism, when the ducks quacked, the pigs grunted? What could be funnier than ducks and pigs anyhow? And to get mention of such things actually in a song made of it the best song one ever heard. This party was marred by one disappointing fly in the ointment. Sandwiches were handed round; and, to my horror, mustard had been smeared on the salt beef. And I didn't like mustard! At least I thought so then; so I came away hungry from that feast!

Yet coming away afforded some solace. Though my home was not five minutes away and to reach it I had not even to leave the well-known pavement, Mr Poppleton sent a big boy—oh such a big boy!—to escort me. It was grand to be trotting along beside so tall a companion! The hour was past nine o'clock. The street lamps were lit; and very few people were about; but I had no provocation for any feeling but my own importance. Mr Poppleton had actually sent Leicester to take care of me! That the school-master looked on me as a little fragile pupil it was good policy to take care of—this never entered my head; and farther away still was the idea which has been taking shape lately, that he may have been rather fond of me.

Not that it need have been fondness exactly—it was more likely curiosity as to the environment of south-English townspeople whose little boys he was teaching—that once prompted him to ask, smiling, "Where did you learn that?" The occasion was unique in my experience;

nothing of the sort ever happened to me before or since; but Mr Poppleton (as if anticipating—for probably he was in fact a little before his time—some more modern piece of "Nature Study") was taking some of us for a walk, "a ramble" as it was afterwards called. Just before Waverley Abbey, we had halted to look at the water in front of Waverley House. On that water was a swan; and by and by I told the others, as we admired the long white neck, "It's got seven bones in its neck." "Where did you learn that?" Mr Poppleton asked. Whether I gave my father or my brother as my authority I don't know now; I don't even know that I was right! The anatomy of swans was not a subject I cared to follow up; and Mr Poppleton himself may have been as ignorant of it as I was and am. Indeed he sometimes failed me; as when he called across the school to Lovey Dovey to listen to a flaw in my composition which stated that rainbows occurred in mornings or afternoons. I knew what I meant, and I ought to have been helped, not jeered at; for it was hardly my own fault that I did not understand how to insert "early" and "late" into the divided sentence. He was not, indeed, invariably fair. It made me feel very sore at the time, when he sneered that one "living under the shadow of the town-clock" (too plainly "me") could not tell anything about winding up the said clock. As if that was my business, any more than his own!

Yet, as I hinted, I am persuaded he was fond of me. At every Christmas and Midsummer "breaking-up," there were prizes for leading boys. Very likely it paid to give prizes, though Mr Poppleton bought them himself. But, at one prize-giving, when I was still too little to have earned anything at all, there was a prize for *me*! Certainly, it did not look so handsome as the books for the big boys—did not reach the level of *Runnymede and Lincoln Fair* and others I took afterwards; to say nothing about a little book by George Catlin about Indians which my brother had once brought home. But then, I had done nothing at all to earn *Pits and Furnaces*, and, as I had no younger brother to follow me, my unlooked-for prize must have been really a present, given because Mr Poppleton liked to please me.

"Specimens"

Many visitors to the sea-side must have seen and sighed over (in their "apartments") uninspired drawings in costly frames on "drawing-room" walls, or texts over bedroom washing-stands, and so on; must have wondered where these embellishments came from and why they were not used for fire-lighting years ago. In fact, these things are singularly precious. They have invaluable associations. Fond parents had them framed and hung up, because, notwithstanding their apparent imbecility, they are the work of some beloved child, clever beyond words. Long afterwards, the child, grown-up to commonplace life at last hesitates to destroy these treasures, because by now, from their place on the wall, their very preservation suggests some father or mother doting but dead. *I* know I used to make such things myself at Mr Poppleton's, and bring them home and think it quite right to have them framed and hung up. At Mr Poppleton's they were called "Specimens," heaven knows why. Only twice a year—that is, before the long holidays—did we do such things, but at these times the whole school was given up to their production. At least every boy not too fumbling had to "do a specimen," and was properly aggrieved if anything interrupted him. Perhaps they were "specimens" of what Mr Poppleton could have taught if he liked; for I don't think my sisters ever did them or could have been shown how at Miss Stratford's. There were two sorts of "Specimens." One sort was simply a large drawing—large enough for a half sheet of cartridge paper. On this we copied suitable drawing copies, using H.B. or even B.B. drawing pencils;—never chalk; and sometimes, with india-rubber, we rubbed a hole through the paper and had to begin again. Heads with long curly locks (one was a child with a smile very hard to draw, nursing a kitten whose fur gave opportunity of bold black-pencil work), long wavy beards, banditti, sleek-maned horses; or again mills and water and trees with woolly foliage, and bridges, and rock-built castles—such were the romantic subjects of the drawing copies from which a specimen might be chosen. "The Sentinel" mentioned in an earlier chapter came into my life in that capacity.

Or there were texts for illuminating. I think quite an industry must have flourished in the preparation of conveniences for this art. Crosses and scrolls and flowers and strange letters all in faint outline and printed on thin white cardboard with directions at the foot as to the colours to be used—these were the substratum; and these were on sale, supplied, perhaps, by the same firm that supplied those tempting circles (about as big as a tea-plate) ready for an artist who wanted to draw a sunset scene. I never knew any boy who could rise to this, but ah! how lovely the circles were, with the blue of heaven shading off into murky distance! Talk of Dutch cheeses! Talk of swedes! For illuminating the texts it was necessary to have a paint-box; because only so could you get the proper white china-ware palette—that oblong dish in shallow and slanting compartments—for mixing three or four different colours. For colours had to be mixed with water, by laborious grinding of a suitable cake of paint from an assortment in a little flat case or tray in another part of the polished cedar paint-box. The cakes of paint were tiny oblongs, very hard, to be held between thumb and fingers while grinding on moistened china-ware. Prussian blue and cobalt and indigo; green bice; crimson lake, vermilion; vandyke brown, sepia—these were in every well-appointed paint-box, and you couldn't get far without a penny lump of gamboge. But gamboge was not to be had in a little oblong cake for grinding, like the other paints. At a chemist's you could buy a lump of it, about as big as a walnut. A wet brush would soon work out lots of its gaudy yellow, until the whole lump was honey-combed with little caverns made by wet brush points. In a mussel shell you might buy for a penny a film—it was little more than that—a mere stain—of gold or silver paint. This, however, was an extravagance. Mr Poppleton himself would do the gilding and silvering, in his spare time. The paint-brushes—a penny each—were of camel-hair; and in buying one you had to suck it, to be sure that it would go properly into a point. In use paint brushes could be sucked clean; and this was often better than rinsing the brush in a teacup full of discoloured water, which took too long to dry away and left no nice point. Between the lips a fine and flexible point could be got to any decent penny brush. Only, you had to be careful not to suck up too much paint. Crimson lake, indeed, tasted delicious; but gamboge was bad and all the green paints were poison. Some of the cakes—an Antwerp Blue I especially remember—did not grind into quite the expected colour all through, but showed a pale and sickly looking inside.

When the specimens were ready, a few days before the holidays, we had to write formal letters home. These served instead of "reports," and always began, "My dear Parents." Of course the device saved Mr Poppleton a deal of labour afterwards, though it must have cost him money. For the letter began on special note-paper, water-lined; and if you made a mess of it, another sheet of paper was supplied, and you began again. Three or four attempts were only to be expected. But at worst it made a useful writing-lesson. The letter home was done in one's best small-hand or copper-plate, with a new pen. "My dear Parents," it ran, "I write to inform you of the progress I have made during the last half year." And so, after de-tailing one's studies, it led up to dates—the date of the beginning of the coming holidays, and then the date of the end of them and the beginning of school in the next quarter.

Quarter, note. The pretentiousness of "terms"—sug-gestive of Eton—was unknown at Mr Poppleton's. The school year being in quarters and half years, we had four sets of holidays; and this plan certainly allowed us the full delights of mid-summer. The holidays were not so long as in modern schools, and the device of "mid-term" holidays was of course unknown; but there was certainly some advantage in having no schooling in the long days.

CHAPTER XXI

BOOKS

AT one period I used to hurry home from morning school so as to have a turn at a certain book that was fascinating me; only, being too hungry to wait for dinner I first provided myself with three or four Osborne biscuits, or, may be, an apple out of the cellar to help pass the time. Thus furnished, I made my way into the Front Room—(probably it was summer; at any rate I was never cold and the sun shone)—and there I settled down to read. Crosswise, with my back lying against one arm of the easy chair near the window, and my knees over the other arm, I had a convenient resting place for what was a thickish book for me in those years—Kingston's *In the Eastern Seas*. Of course the age for *Buds and Blossoms* had gone by; and I had failed to get any real pleasure out of many attempts to read my sister's poetry book. We learnt no poetry at Mr Poppleton's;—it possibly seemed to me a girl's subject, though I have no recollection of thinking so, or of despising it. But with good-will enough, I could not really like "Paine's Poetry." "Oh call my brother back to me, I cannot play alone," was altogether too heart-rending; the least hint of losing my brother was not to be borne. "I am coming, I am coming, Hark the busy bee is humming," may have stood for Spring; it had no charms for me. "The Arab to his favourite steed" was of course noble as the matchless animal itself, with the "proudly arched and glossy neck" and all; but I seldom got to the end of the verses—they took too long a time. "Web-spinner" was grimy; "Will you walk into my parlour" offensive; and "John Barleycorn" was not much better. "The Fakenham Ghost" ought to have pleased but somehow didn't; in fact, Poetry was dull stuff. On the other hand, I was just ripe for the excitement to be got from adventure books, and for this there was but one other book to match *In the Eastern Seas*. No; it was not another Kingston; though that author had not yet surfeited me[1], nor had this other book any ravishing wood-cuts of palm-fringed atolls or of sunsets over waste ocean horizons, with flying fish or lonely sea-birds. It could not, like *In the Eastern Seas*, set me chuckling at Mr Tarbox, or exulting at the magnanimity of Mr Thuddicumb; but, on the other hand, a new set of experiences, new scenes, new animals and exploits, sent me again and again to Campbell's *The Old Forest Ranger*. Here too I was just ready for the book. I was old enough to suck a sort of flavour from its pages; not yet old enough (as when I tasted them lately) to smile at the airs of the Sahibs who figured in all the scenes, or to be nauseated by their magnificent "big-game" butchery. On the contrary, I liked it all—liked reading about tigers and salaaming "natives," and the Neilgherry Hills, and the exploits of Mansfield, and the comical drunkenness of "The Doctor." *The*

[1] A year or two later, at the Grammar School, I did tell another boy that Kingston's curious grammar put me off from his works. The other boy stoutly maintained that for him grammar didn't matter if the story was good, whereas I, for my part, sincerely enough felt that a writer ought not to fob one off with English faulty even to schoolboy ears. I don't think I was priggish about it. Expressions like "Between you and I" did really make me wince.

Old Forest Ranger almost worked magic on my imagination. Was that merely a yard at East Street, sloping up behind the wheelwright's shop? No Indian jungle could have been thicker with adventure. Those two or three dirty elm stocks which the blacksmiths used in some of their work with wheels—were they not really wild boars? Turned on their sides, they might seem to lumber woodenly down the slope, but they really charged, savagely—unless checked with a spear something like a broken pole from the neighbouring hop-ground. With this apparatus "Pig-sticking" was indeed as delightful a sport for me as for Charles in the book. Nor was it in sport only that I resembled him. I had an iron hoop with as good a right to be called "Challenger" as his mettlesome pony. My Challenger also was swift. It took me miles. In short, *The Old Forest Ranger*, though I didn't much like it the other day, was just my clip when I was ten years old.

Of course there were other books. *A Thousand Miles in the Rob Roy Canoe* (I forget the author—was it a Mr Gregory?) had interesting pages though not all of it could be read. The same may be said of *The Country Year Book*, and Gerstaeker's *Wild Sports in the Far West*. *Near Home* and *Far Off* were a sort of school book, offensively informative. Wood's *Natural History* was precious for a reason to be told later; and for another reason, equally valid, I liked *Common Objects of the Country* and *Common Objects of the Sea Shore*. Figuier's *Mammalia* (a Christmas present to my brother) had ravishing pictures—especially a lion's head in profile; and I could find a good deal to read in *Evenings at Home*, and in *The Magnet Stories*,

Beeton's Annual, Old Merry's Annual, a volume of *Chatter-box,* and not a few other books. A little cheap copy, in a limp green cover, of *Tom Brown's Schooldays* was as good to have (and to read again and again) as *Eric, or Little by Little* (tried soon afterwards) was objectionable and insulting to boyhood. There were indeed several books I disliked—"goody-goody" books especially; and I never took to books with unattractive pages or ugly pictures. *Strewelpeter* did not amuse; and if it had not been for "Phiz" I might have sampled Dickens then (to be like Harry East in "Tom Brown") instead of turning away with distaste from volumes that rather repelled me until I was near twenty. I liked A.L.O.E. The title of *The Lake in the Woods* was a romance in itself. *Ned Franks* had a sub-title which I called "The Christian's Panalopy." The "a" indeed improved the taste of that mouthful of a word and anyhow I envied Ned Franks's ability to paint (with one hand too—I couldn't do it myself with two) all the flags of all the navies of the world. Another book there was that was all the better for an "a" I supplied myself— Holme Lee's Fairy Tales. For, by no means suspecting frivolity with the name I revered, the hero of the book seemed to me to be called Tuflongabo—it would have spoilt all the magic that clung to him to call him Tough-Long-Bow. Besides, I had never heard of "drawing the long bow." Other book names I recall were *The Orphans and Old Poz, Beechnut, The Crofton Cousins* (it told of a ride in a carriage a mile long, and I despised the clumsy phrasing). *A Trap to catch a Sunbeam* seemed an ingenious title; *Old Friends and New Friends* always pleased. Lamb's

Tales from Shakespeare, and also a collection of Aesop's Fables, could not be read in the type of the duodecimo edition, which was what I had got. Similarly I refused to read the double columns of a truly sumptuous *Robinson Crusoe* which had been given to my brother for a Christmas present. The tempting coloured plates could not prevail against the ugliness of the pages.

Of course the newspaper shop was a help. At some misguided moment my father—not choosing what might attract customers or library readers, who indeed never came; but pleasing solely his own uninstructed tastes—had filled a small shelf with books that no one wanted, amongst which was a thick volume called *Waterton's Wanderings*. It had illustrations—a blow pipe I think and, certainly, a peccary. I could not put up with most of the book, it bored me so badly. But all it had to tell about peccaries I read again and again. The shop of course furnished current magazines—*The Child's Companion*, *Little Folks* (a godsend at that period), *The Sunday at Home*. On the cover of this last publication, amidst little woodcuts which I felt to be rather namby-pamby, was one odd legend: "The Child is Father of the Man." How could that be? I asked my father sometimes and he could make it seem reasonable; but I never could remember his explanation for many days together. Probably none of my mother's customers subscribed to *Punch*—I do not remember seeing it. Of the cheaper "comics," *Fun* was possibly the less objectionable, but it looked rubbishy. *Judy* may just be remembered as the originator of *Ally Sloper* and his friend *Iky Mo*. It was probably later that one of the Bishops seen in Farnham Streets was held to look not unlike Ally Sloper.

Mention must be made of *The Animal World*. My mother, none too expensively educated herself, was always on the watch for influences she approved; and while she never scolded or punished me, it must have been to her that I owed every week the quiet and unnoticed growth of feelings fostered by *The Animal World*. Never anywhere else did I read about Rarey and Race-horses, or the infamy of the bearing-rein. And I think it was under the same influence—my mother's influence—that I became the proud possessor of lovely books: *Animal Sagacity*, *Clever Dogs and Horses*, *Our Faithful Friends*. These books were lovely because their ornate covers were embellished, each of them, with a coloured circular print—a horse or a dog—let into the cloth; while Harrison Weir was the illustrator of almost every page.

CHAPTER XXII

DRAWING

It has been told how, on the morning when I played truant from Miss May's school, it seemed good to me to pass the time at drawing; the copy—a basket of eggs in *Mavor's Spelling Book*—never had any great attraction that I remember; only, there it was—something to draw—and I copied it slavishly, even imitating the very size—an inch or so square. There seems to have been enjoyment for me in the mere exercise of eyes and fingers; I had no idea of making pictures. This was probably the period when I used my left hand to draw spiky mountains on my slate. I sometimes drew plans—as much as three inches by two, perhaps—of Farnham Streets. In a little book, that seems to have disappeared, were gummed diminutive drawings from Wood's *Natural History*—a stickle-back, a jerboa (I loved jerboas because they seemed like little child-made things), besides fancy drawings of lions and tigers (very many or very stripy) and elephants, all as they ought to be. According to my drawing elephants would have proudly arched necks much as self-respecting Arab horses should have, only more so, elephants being nobler animals even than horses. In my drawings, their heads mounted on necks making a quarter of a circle at the back, where a horse would have a mane.

A time soon came when I was ambitious of something more pictorial; as is proved by a pencil drawing (on a half sheet of note paper) of a donkey—from *Mavor's Spelling*

Book again. This, though only a copy, was quite pretentious in size and finish and all. Admiring it immensely, I could not wait before showing it to my grandfather—taking precautions first to prepare him for a yet more dazzling finish. "Not Dun Yet" the drawing is marked in print letters, then comes my name, followed by the date, and the proud announcement that I was six years old. Truly, it was well to let my grandfather be under no delusion on this important matter. He would ask me sometimes how tall I was going to be, and I would answer "As tall as the ceiling." There was always an appreciative twinkle of laughter about this dialogue, as though each of us knew it to be partly fun, but in serious matters, like my amazing cleverness, it was as well that there should be no room for error.

Probably I had flattery enough to make me very conceited. I don't know when I went to the School of Art; but I cannot have been far past ten, if I was as old as that, when I began. The School of Art was a new thing in Farnham. One long low room at the top of the Town Hall Building was its home—not many steps, in fact, from our shop. It required almost as many steps to climb up to that garret from the street. The room devoted to art was a glory hole. A few of Brucciani's casts stood up amidst the litter—drawing boards, desks spared from the Corn Exchange downstairs; a few "registers," drawing pins, mouldy objects for "still-life" study—a penny ink-bottle, a stove, plentiful fragments of dry bread. In summer one could look out of window down into the Borough, or across the street into the upper rooms of the opposite houses, seeing especially one old lady much esteemed in Farnham, but not to be seen otherwise, since she never went down-stairs. In winter, any absence of the master, Mr Offord, gave opportunity, speedily taken, for a "bread-fight"; the evening students excitedly pelting one another with more or less stale bread left by young ladies of the after-noon class. Foremost in these "fights" was Jim Offord, the master's son—a merry youth about twice my age, whom I much admired. Whether he could draw or not I don't know, but I had no doubt he was very clever in all ways. Athletic too. Had I not watched him, in the very first football game—Rugby football—played in Farnham Park by the newly formed club? Was he not also "engaged" to the local platform-singing young lady? Above all, was not his father the wonderful Mr Offord?

I revered—I almost worshipped—Mr Offord. It is true, I had seen one greater man—Mr Hook, the R.A. from Churt, who sometimes appeared in his waggonette in Farnham streets, wrapped up in a shawl—or perhaps it was a plaid and I knew that Mr Hook had something to do with the School of Art and with Mr Offord's appoint-ment. But the R.A. was altogether too remote, whereas Mr Offord—a very kind and very human being as I found—was an Artist who could be approached.

I had no suspicion then that he might be struggling to make both ends meet, or that he was possibly a muddler, not too capable of managing business. I once saw him tie a steel nib to a broken penholder and make shift with that rather than get a new holder. And I thought it clever.

How was I to realise that there might be a pathetic if not tragic significance to such make-shifts? I don't remember that he ever tried to keep order—or that he had any provocation to try. We liked him, and were proud to please him—at least, I was proud. If the place was untidy —as it doubtless was—I never heard of a caretaker to help keep it clean. But certainly any idea of such a thing being necessary was far from me. To me it was proud joy to stand beside him and gloat over his ingenious preparation of a new drawing-copy forme. Doubling my half-sheet of cartridge paper, he got a perpendicular straight line in the middle of the paper and quickly pencilled the left-hand side of any design that came into his head; it being for me then to draw the reverse side. After some months of this sort of exercise I was allowed to begin "shading from the cast"—hands, feet, bas-relief panels of pomegranate or of egg-plant. The bust of the Venus of Milo, Apollo, Diomede (his nose always looked dusty), Clytie, the face of Michael Angelo's Moses, a complete and full-sized "Fighting Gladiator"—these were drawn later. The School had been moved then into its present building, and other casts were added; yet it seems to me that it was partly in contemplation of these first casts that I began to delight in shapely surfaces. At no other school did I acquire anything so well worth having as the habit of reverence gradually fostered in me by the Venus of Milo. The muscles of a Discobolus, later, helped me to the same lesson that I was learning, all unconsciously, from the contours of the sparrow's skull, the shepherd's crown. Shape, well adapted—that was the thing to care for. I thought it "Art"; but I was very young, and for years there was nobody to correct my thoughts.

Once Mr Offord took hold of my hand (his own hands were large and plump) and admired its childish smallness, as if affectionately. But it was only my priggishness that fed on that kindly act. And I was awfully priggish— vanity all through. At Mr Poppleton's there was another little boy who could draw; of course not so well as I could! That was unthinkable; still, he had some slight talent. So one day I planned out a future for him and me. I was going to be a great R.A., like Mr Hook; he—my little friend—was going to be a School of Art master, like Mr Offord, under me. The funny thing is, Jimmy seemed pleased. He was not big enough to punch my head.

Truly, my ambitions were not hampered by modesty. My model then—the very greatest man who ever lived —was Sir Edwin Landseer. Ansdell, Herring, Rosa Bonheur, may have had some merit; but they were as nothing beside the painter of "Dignity and Impudence." Landseer's great work however would be carried on by me. Probably Harrison Weir's drawings kindled some of this enthusiasm—possibly *The Animal World*. Animals were the loveliest things on earth.

Still, other things attracted me; and since by now I definitely meant to "be" an artist, of course it was de- sirable to perfect my great skill in drawing. Mr Offord could only help me on School of Art nights. Guidance at other times was sought occasionally in *Vere Foster's Draw- ing Books*. Taste too—the right taste—had to be found. In this matter—as in so many others (ah! so many) my

brother gave me a lead. In the Library of "The Young
Men's Association" he had found many bound volumes
of the *Art Journal*, and by and by we could not be satiated
with steel engravings of pictures, some of which it was a
simple duty to admire. So I admired them. How I learnt
what I ought to like would not be easy to say now;
fortunately, beneath each engraving was the artist's name,
which I soon learnt to see in a jiffy. A rapturous "Oh-h"
followed—almost before the engraving had been glanced
at. Enough, if one detected the great name. So I fostered
my taste for J. M. W. Turner, and soon knew enough to
despise Claude Lorraine. Constable was passable, yet he
was not in it with Turner. An occasional Clarkson Stan-
field or Hobbema or more modern painter exercised no
discrimination in saying "Oh." Landseer turned up sometimes—always to be worshipped—and of course I soon
knew enough to admire Raphael or Rembrandt.

The odd thing is, that a genuine delight in pictures took
root and grew in this sham admiration. Perhaps it came
from the act of looking; for, knowing that Raphael had
got to be admired, it was just as well to discover if one
could what the charm was. And sometimes one was rewarded by a little success. So insincerity may lead to its
opposite. It is comforting to realise this in these days,
when youthful enthusiasts gush over the latest fashion in
painting, in music, in literature. Something may come
of it.

CHAPTER XXIII

VISITS

AMONGST memories of being a petted but happy little chap, there is one that sees me with my Aunt Sarah starting off to walk to Runfold, to Mrs Robert Baker's. Of that expedition nothing remains definite enough to be set down here, save only the rapture of passing by a nurseryman's garden, where snow-drops were nodding up gaily from amidst snow. Evidently it was a joyful February morning. The trees were adrip, sunshine gleamed. Plump wet drops glistened and splashed; the snow was going; Spring was coming. In another memory, Summer has come, sumptuous, lazy, splendid. This time it is afternoon—lovely endless afternoon, tree-shadowed, in a slanting meadow with orchard, at Spreakley near Frensham. Others are about—numbers of them, cousins I think, and some seniors, and from the leisureliness, the warm-limbed comfort, the cool-looking dresses, the laughing good-temper, the easy-going provincial talk, it seems to have been in Herrick's time. Cows were prospering somewhere near that high grass; and it was there I tasted syllabub, for the first and last time in my life. I don't know that I liked syllabub much, but in Herrick's day it is right to sample country things.

With Aunt Sarah again I sometimes walked to Wrecclesham, where her sister, my Aunt Baker, and my Uncle John Baker, had a farm. There, probably with my own sister Mary and my brother, I had the huge delight of sucking milk through a straw. Once I went across the road from there to the village dressmaker, and was impressed by the soft-looking and wavy smoothness of her brown hair over her temples. I had never seen hair worth notice before. That same evening, on my way home to Farnham, Aunt Sarah took me in to her friend Mrs Hatch's, somewhere near the cemetery, and, in Mrs Hatch's room, so intense was the quiet of the sleepy summer afternoon that the ticking of a clock then sometimes returns to my memory to this day. I cannot remember the clock itself; but I am not sorry to be reminded sometimes of its arresting but unceasing tick, so calm yet calling attention to the passing of the afternoon.

Another clock I remember was Aunt Mary's cuckoo-clock, or rather her husband Uncle Albert's; but that was far away at Camberwell. I liked it well enough—liked to see the cuckoo come out of his little door and stand cuckooing. But my brother was old enough to know that cuckoo-clocks were not the thing, so of course I could not admire it much. One cannot admire much, when an elder brother is flippant. It was probably because of my trouble with asthma that my mother took me so often with her, when her shop required a visit to wholesale places in London. The business could not be got through in a day; and as I often needed her help at night I accompanied my mother to her sister's at Camberwell. I liked my Aunt Mary very much. She had a funny way of puckering up her features to express the appropriate emotion while she talked, and leaving the grimace unchanged when the talk it illustrated had quite changed. So, she might be still frowning with sorrow when it was time to laugh, or wearing puzzled eyebrows after the enlightenment had come. But, knowing her to be always kind—kind as my own mother herself—and full of fun, I always liked going to Aunt Mary's. I liked the change of scene, and especially the change of food.

Always there was a soda cake for tea; and nobody else but Aunt Mary ever made soda cake. Then there was different bread and butter. At tea, Uncle Albert once told how new bakers' carts were to be seen all about the streets, selling Neville's bread. I don't know whether that was the bread we were then having. Where we went about London I cannot even guess. I have a dim recollection of seeing St Paul's, in an otherwise unapproachable view from a back room in some warehouse; a still dimmer recollection —a faint belief rather—of being acquainted with the knife-board of an omnibus. The Thames too I must have seen, or Uncle Baker would not have teased me afterwards, pretending that "The Barge River" or "The Row-barge" —the Basingstoke Canal at Aldershot—was as big as the tremendous Thames of my boasts. So ignorant of him! We also went to a draper's shop—Messrs Tarn's— crowded, I think, with Christmas shoppers, and disappointing to me because there were no toys. Toys, though, we did see in plenty at the Lowther Arcade; and there we bought a present—a box of bricks—for my brother at home. The Arcade whirred where shop assistants were spinning tops, winding up squeaking dolls, sending toy-traffic or mechanical mice across the pavement— themselves—men or women—walking about amongst their marvellous stock looking as discontented as caged animals.

Real caged animals I probably saw at the Zoo. It must have been on one of these occasions also that we paid that visit to the Polytechnic already told of in an earlier chapter. We went to the Crystal Palace, too, where I was chiefly interested in the models, so lifelike, of Red Indians in forests, and of alligators basking beside the ponds in the grounds. That, and a gallery holding many mechanical devices, fascinated me. Only, it was tiresome of the grown-ups, who knew how to get pennies, to refuse so obtusely to drop a second penny in the slot and see again the little navvies begin to wheel their wheel-barrows up and down, and in and out.

At one time my father must have joined us at one of these visits to Camberwell. With Uncle Albert, he took me (and I fancy my brother was of the party) to Kew Gardens. We went by the Underground Railway, and it was part of the wonder of the expedition to be travelling on a summer day, through a gloomy and smoky tunnel, with nothing but a dingy lamp to see the way. I enjoyed all that. Kew Gardens was more interesting to my father than to me. In a room of a house called a museum a glass case contained some half-finished wooden animals, just like the toy horses and dogs I had at home. These carvings came from Switzerland. But the little interest they may have had for me was swamped by an altercation my father had out of doors, with one of the gardeners. The man ordered my father back from some short cut he was taking across the grass, and there were high words. It disturbed me to hear my father spoken to like that, but it amused Uncle Albert. He seemed to know the man's name, referred to him as "Mike," and often laughed a joyful chuckling laugh afterwards as if he saw something funny in the affair. At Camberwell I heard talk of Newman Hall, and of Spurgeon. Later, at Brixton, we went to a Presbyterian Chapel, and another time to an Independent Church and the Boys' Brigade.

I once stayed a night at my Uncle Richard's at Millbridge. A neighbour came in and we had some singing that evening. Everybody was very kind to me. One of my cousins showed me how to play back-gammon (but I thought it a dull pastime) and had a game with me. There was abundance of my uncle's fruit, and then—then followed a dreadful night. Happily for me, my mother was there to take care of me. I was not sick, but I guess that my digestive organs had ceased to function. Asthma suffocated me all night, and next day we came home. The places where I could not sleep were growing in number, and further experiments were not to be encouraged.

One other experiment, however, we did make; although at Uncle Richard's a night's rest was now as impossible for me as I was wont to find it at Farnborough at Christmas. My father's other brother lived too far away. But his sister Mary—my Aunt Baker—need not be avoided. I think it was after, but it may have been before, the Wrecclesham episode already mentioned; anyhow Uncle and Aunt Baker had a farm near Bentley Station—from one side of the house you could see across a paddock to the village shop and the turnpike road between Farnham and Alton—and there my mother took me to stay, perhaps more than once. My uncle was probably very busy—no memories of him remain—but Aunt Baker seems almost visible now. Small, skinny, with sunken jaws (teeth gone, it may be supposed). She was merry all the time, her thin face one wide-mouthed smile and her mischievous eyes all a-dance. Vivacity embodied—that's what she seems to have been, without doubt full of the one aim of giving my father's wife and youngster a joyful time.

And I, for my part, enjoyed it. A little walled-in enclosure in the garden—low wall of bricks half grey with lichen—was full of gooseberry bushes and weeds—so weedy that Aunt Baker called it, as if that was oh such fun, "The Wilderness." But I liked having the run of the gooseberry crop. About the rest of the garden all I can remember is narrow gravelly straight walks, and no shade anywhere. The little gravel stones glistened, and looked hard and pitiless. Out in the farm was shade, behind a "stump" of old hay; and there, one afternoon (I am sure I was with my brother at that time), it startled me when two small Highland oxen came trotting round and stopped short—surprised to find boys there. They looked harmless little things, at any rate my brother seemed not to mind them. I have often wondered at the name for them—"Scotch Runts"—which we must have got from Uncle Baker. Although he is not in any memories I have of that farm, he cannot but have been one of the party that day—it was probably some business affair of his own—

when we walked in "The Holt" (Alice Holt—dapple of leaf-shade and sunlight) and I was ravished by a small feather, with blue patches. A jay's feather someone said it was.

There, at Bentley, I had a guinea-fowl's egg—very rich, with golden yolk—for breakfast. No doubt there was always plenty of food. An ancient picture of a harvest waggon pleased me. In a scarcity of books, *Enquire Within upon Everything* was a stand-by. A section in it given over to riddles was a Godsend to a little boy eager to seem clever when company came; though the only company that did come while I was at Bentley was two middle-aged maiden ladies from a neighbouring farm, who seemed stupidly indifferent to riddles. They came to tea one afternoon; another afternoon we went to a fête at the Rectory, where the Rector's son—a biggish boy— seemed to be "showing off." He took part in a game at "Bob-cherry" unknown to me elsewhere; and I think too I tried my hand at "trap-bat." Yet another outing was at a fête at Froyle Park. Not a vestige of memory remains of that affair except that name. But that evening, after we got back, Aunt Baker, not fatigued, grew merrier than ever, as if delighting to make me laugh. For her own laughing eyes twinkled at mine, while, picking up her skirts each side with thumb and finger, she did a sort of clog-dance in front of me, singing "Jim Crow's Sister Had a Wooden Leg"—a poem of which I know no more now than that it ended with a boisterous spondaic "Jump! Jim Crow!"

But one afternoon we went to tea at Isington Mill, and

a few pleasant details of that expedition are almost vivid in my memory. Not the Lucases themselves who kept the mill; every recollection of them save their name has quite faded out. But the comely walled-in garden where we had tea seems clear. Such a warm welcome of rich sunshine and green grass could not help lasting. The grass was a narrow though longish strip between a gravelled pathway and the little quiet old river Wey. The path—our chairs and the tea-table stood on it—had started from the house and the mill, all forgotten now; but it ended just behind us in a summer-house that held lots of interesting things and an air of limitless leisure. Two or three balls were handed round, like smallish cricket balls of pale brown tint; and they were said to be—what I never saw before nor since—balls of hair taken from the stomachs of horses, that had the fatal habit of licking one another. The fancy thus conjured up, of country horses and quiet pasture—the whole association with mill and peaceful lane—made it quite agreeable to see and handle these things; so that even now I think of them with liking for what they suggested to me. But most of all I enjoy remembering sundry very beautiful objects brought out for our inspection from shelves or hooks in that English summer-house—shining clubs and paddles, of savages in South-sea Islands or Australia. They belonged to some Lucas or other—I never understood or greatly cared who he was—but to this day I treasure some charm they yielded to me then. One little round-knobbed club there was I remember especially. The paddles—a dark brown—had strange carvings incised, in rows all across the blades, in rings round the handles; but this little deadly club, less ornate, seemed polished and shone brown like a horse-chestnut newly dropped and split out of its shell; and instead of savagery its glistening colours told then of a peaceful English garden and a lovely summer afternoon. They have not done telling me that.

CHAPTER XXIV

AT THE SEASIDE

My very first diary—I am tempted to write " 1st "—began with a date—June 1874—and went on "Came to Bognor. Saw the sea for the 1st time." This was in a diminutive pocket book of cream-laid paper—a book lost long ago. It had been obtained for the purpose of recording that unprecedented adventure to the seaside, and I read it often enough to be able to recall the opening. The exact date which it gave escapes me, but plainly I was about eleven years old at the time. Believing it to be proper that a diary should consist of unpremeditated and therefore laconic jottings I purposely began in that jumpy style; and seeing that the writing was done with soft lead pencil, and the paper was smooth, it may be supposed that the pages grew smudgy. But I wish I could see the book again, to freshen my memory of what proved to be a more momentous holiday than I was capable of knowing then.

To go back a little—Bognor was not what had been intended. Ventnor had been spoken of, and lodgings actually secured there; and I have recollection of a certain fireside Sunday evening which must have been in the spring of 1874, when my mother was explaining the odd word "chine," with reference to Shanklin Chine. Incidentally, it should be said that this was, almost certainly, all new to my mother herself. She may have seen the sea once—from Southampton—in her girlhood; but I think she had never had a holiday; and if her mind was all afire with this prospect it would be a pleasant thing to me now to fancy it. But it is likelier that she had studied up this matter of "chines" chiefly for the sake of preparing us children for keener enjoyment. After that, the prospect of a change for herself may have brought her some secondary pleasure. Lodgings as aforesaid were booked. We were to go in the midsummer holidays. And then a bitter blow! The project had to be given up, however much my mother may have counted on it. We could not go to Ventnor. One of my father's customers, owing about £40, failed to pay, and had to call a meeting of his creditors. £40 was not a small sum to a family like ours; yet, so far as I remember, the only complaint in our household referred to the further pound or so that had to be paid as compensation to the owner of the rooms at Ventnor. Certainly I for one had no real disappointment to lament. Of course it would have been nice to see the sea; but after all I didn't need any additional happiness. My normal life was satisfying enough. My mother had much more reason to be disappointed; but it is most unlikely that she owned it. That would have vexed my father too much. He too might have liked a holiday after so many years; and he must have hated to have been a spoil-sport.

What happened next I do not know; probably the defaulting debtor was able to offer a better composition than had been hoped for, and my father and mother were able to return to a part of the discarded plan, although Ventnor had been given up. At any rate the next thing I remember is hearing a railway porter call out "Barnham! Change for Bognor," and then being in a little room at Bognor, looking across the road to the parade and a level blue horizon above it and wondering what that queer rattling noise could be from just beyond the parade. I soon found that it was the scream of shingle drawn back by spent waves. Whether I had, that lovely summer afternoon, eyes to see, no doubt I had a nose to smell the bed of red carnations just under the open window in the front of our lodgings; but there was much else to look at. The parade was paved with pale bricks—pink and yellow; and on the further edge of it, near the beach, was a long row, stretching into the distance, of tarred wickerwork objects— lobster pots, I learnt. The pier, a little to the right, had whitewashed posts—or were they tarred? There were probably many boats out, on the blue summer Channel, but I have no recollection of them. Neither have I any recollection of looking at the sea, or of watching the tide going down. The whole thing was in fact too far beyond my experience to have any meaning for me or any attraction.

Meanings were not slow to come. It was probably the next morning that, from far across the beach, I was aware of my mother calling. With my brother or my sister I had followed down to watch the surf on that level sand; and my mother was in an agony of fear lest the tide should race back too hurriedly. How was she to know? Such things were possible on some shores. Once reassured though, she never tired of watching the steady rise or fall of tide, as the waves, now here, now there, gained or perhaps lost more yards of the wide sand.

And that sand itself; what a wonder it was! To watch

the innumerable ripple marks, or to look at the worm-
casts dotted all over it, or to see round one's feet the dry
surface grow wet and shiny and even squashy under one's
weight! From the shingle, when the tide was high enough,
one could make "ducks and drakes" out across the restless
water. A flat stone could always be found. My fingers grew
rough and my arm stiff with continuous stone-throwing.

Wherever one turned the sand was alive with tiny crabs,
its own colour and no bigger then spiders, the month being
June. And all along the beach, for miles perhaps, were the
thin lines—"little windrows" as Walt Whitman called
them—of seaweed, dainty and worth keeping an eye on
for treasures to take home for my museum. Strange things
the sea cast up; and a strange collection began to fill our
chiffonier drawer, until soon the said drawer had a stale
dry smell, like the hot shingle itself. Plentiful amongst
the pebbles—the brown and sometimes grey pebbles—
along with water-worn oyster shells and cockle shells and
fragments of large scallops, were pretty little nut-brown
and red spiral shells of the "netted dog-whelk." I did not
realise that these must be as much effaced as the others.
Their shape pleased me, and I did a careful drawing of one
in my new diary. Moreover, under the drawing I wrote
the name, and even the Latin name—"*Nassa Reticulata.*"
Was that right? I never questioned it until now, but felt
proudly learned. Where I found the name I do not know.
Perhaps I had brought some book that informed me, or
perhaps I got it from my brother. The thing was as new
to him as to me; but he had a habit of finding out and
omitting to speak unless he was asked.

From unknown sources too a sort of enlightenment, satisfying then at least, came in explanation of other mysteries. It almost sufficed for explanation if a name could be got; for a name does indeed make further enquiry possible. And names at least, that might be corrected, were forthcoming. I now learned to call "cuttle bone" a beauteous snow-white thing quite unknown to me. On Bognor sands these comely and curved shapes were fairly common—about the size and shape of a boot sole—and I never passed a specimen without an almost conscious admiration of its leaf-like contours and some dim idea of a function I supposed it to serve. And then there were odd black things about as big as a flattened match-box, with an extension at each corner—things made, as it looked, of brittle and thick black tissue paper—"sharks' eggs," somebody said they were. "Dog-fish's eggs" there were too, longer, narrower—half transparent gelatine, the colour of the sand, with rounded corners and spiral tendrils tangled into the seaweed. It was intriguing to see these shapes. Cockle shells, razor shells, whelk shells containing long-legged hermit crabs, all added to the fascination. The seaweed was a joy in itself—branched, small, frondy, in brilliant pink or green or warm brown. I collected many different seaweeds, but could get no names for them, and lost interest; for without names, how was I to make a show of knowledge?

As if my mother might otherwise be too free of care, my sister was taken ill with measles at Bognor. The water at Bognor was more briny than she could endure; and from Farnham some of the sweet home water was sent by Aunt

Ann, or brought by my father, who if he did not travel with us, must have joined us later. Certainly he was at Bognor during a part of our holiday. One day, not unwilling perhaps to get us out of my mother's way, he took the rest of us to Brighton. I ought not to have been allowed to go. I ought to have been smacked and sent to bed, for it is probable I had been eating greedily; and that morning I had a sick headache. But I insisted on joining the Brighton party. Without question I was too naughty—too much the disagreeable spoilt child—to be left behind to add to my mother's cares just then. In a restaurant at Brighton my father had to take me downstairs into the back premises, and there I was abominably sick. Still, we got down to the shingle eventually. At each groyne shingle was piled deep on one side, and was very much lower on the other side, quite unlike Bognor, where things were arranged so much better. And ultimately we went into the Aquarium. There it probably interested me—who knew chiefly minnows in the Wey—to see large fish. Yet the only thing I can remember seeing was sea-horses—right enough in shape of head, but disappointingly small. When a thing was called "horse" ought it not to have been bigger than one's finger?

One other thing about my father comes back to my memory—one solitary thing—during that Bognor holiday —his delight at finding that he still could swim. For that was long before the day of public swimming baths, and Farnham "River" was still available for boys only. Not for twenty years, my father said, had he tried to swim; and it gladdened him at Bognor to find that he still had the art.

He did not know then that some things, like the growth and arrangement of muscular fibres, do not perish easily, as if they were memories of thought alone.

We lodged in a little, sunny, very unpretentious place long ago gone, which was the home of a fisherman and his wife. The fisherman, unless my memory is quite wrong, was a large-faced sandy-haired old chap, with one peculiarity my brother and I noticed, though I rarely noticed such things. This old fisherman, bumbly, fumbly, had a queer way of wearing his ample trousers braced so low that there seemed no length of thigh above his knee. He looked all trousers. But he was a laughing, waddling, jolly old chap, and we liked him. Unfortunately, and quite innocently, he added a good deal to my mother's fears, when he proposed to take my brother out with him fishing. My mother would not hear of it. Ready to face every fear that was within her own power to control, she would not face risks for my brother with somebody else, and she refused the fisherman's offer. He was terribly offended; but that made no difference.

Meanwhile, a great thing was happening to me. I was making a new friendship. Years—more than four years—made my brother a little too old to be my constant companion; but there was at Bognor at the same time with us another family from Farnham—Mr and Mrs Nichols, with their son Arthur. We had hardly known one another before; but now intimacy ripened, and it was destined to last. Especially it grew into a passionate friendship between Arthur and me. In passing, I may mention that he, my first friend, grew to be as lovable a man as I ever met.

At Bognor we soon became inseparable. What was there we did not do together? I remember one baking summer afternoon—nobody was about, because dinner was hardly over—but in a bit of unfrequented road on the way to Arthur's lodgings, the grass amongst the loose stones, with wide-open pimpernels too, was getting dry and yellow in the steady heat, and I rejoiced in it because I was soon to meet Arthur. I gloat, remembering that roadful of hot sunshine pouring down on the grass, beating up from the stones, and nobody about, so silent.

Arthur wore a puggaree—a piece of muslin twisted round his straw hat, with ends hanging down behind to keep the sun off his nape; so I had to have a puggaree too, my experience of the sea being younger than his, though I was the older by two or three years. We paddled together. Sometimes as we splashed through the comfortable sun gleaming water, a little flat fish—a sole, I supposed—the colour of the sand—darted past my feet. I do not think it was at Bognor that Arthur showed me acorn shells clustered on the timbers of the pier. We certainly saw no sea-anemones there, and there may or may not have been shrimps, or winkles and limpets on a few rocks to the westward. We found starfish, jelly fish, a dead octopus or two. With Arthur, I did help his mother pick up stones from the shingle to take to a lapidary in the town; and after the man had put them all aside as worthless for polishing, no doubt I helped take them back to the beach.

I wish I could give a lifelike account of Mrs Nichols— rather a new type to me—but that would be to restore the very essence of Farnham middle-class comfort and respectability fifty years ago. Well-to-do (not rich), a little self-indulgent, a little like a spoilt child in fact—plump, scrupulously honest and truthful, neighbourly, kind— nay, tender-hearted almost beyond measure—fond of tasty food, full of laughing good temper—Mrs Nichols is to be remembered with much affection. And it helps the affection that she took such a liking for my mother even to the extent of looking up to her with admiration. Compared to my mother Mrs Nichols had an easy time of it, though she was not idle—at least she occupied herself with domestic duties—but she was certainly true-hearted; a genuine friend. Her superior command of money made no difference to her manner—the manner of a comfortable English middle-class churchwoman of the mid-Victorian era.

But all this of course was not in the thoughts of the child I was then. For Arthur's sake I liked his mother and father; and it seemed only natural and reasonable that good feeling should exist between them and my own mother and father. How was I to guess that the whole of my future would be affected by this intimacy? None the less, that is what happened.

Though our holiday lasted but a fortnight, my friendship with Arthur Nichols continued and strengthened after we had got back to Farnham. Moreover, within a year the Nicholses had offered, and my father and mother had gladly accepted, the tenancy of an old family book and stationery shop Mr Nichols owned at 42 Borough. The house was roomier—and we had begun to need more room—and the shop too would admit of extension of business which had been beyond my mother's reach before. In short, while 18 Borough had been only a little poky tenement, on the other hand 42 Borough was an opening to considerable middle-class comfort. The change was decidedly an advantage for us.

One other change there had been, making more possible the Bognor holiday and its consequences. At East Street my grandfather had died, a month or two after Uncle John, the cripple, the house having been altered for Aunt and Uncle Baker from Bentley. Though I don't think my grandfather's death meant any great increase of income for my father, it may well have meant freedom from criticism. I never heard hint of it indeed, yet I think it likely my grandfather would disapprove of holidays—even as his son, my Uncle Richard, did years afterwards. In his own old age, Uncle Richard exclaimed "I can't think what you want to go away for!" to any of his family asking for a little relaxation. He himself had fitted so closely into the environing countryside—one cannot any longer get such intimacy with one's environment (I, for one, have never been into the country in that intense way); and it is likely enough that my grandfather would have taken umbrage if his shop and business had seemed slighted by my father. But the old man was gone. He no longer had to be considered. My father was free—and able to let us see more of the world than just Farnham.

CHAPTER XXV

ANOTHER CHANGE

WITHIN a year after the Bognor holiday a discontent arose amongst the boys of Mr Poppleton's school. I know so little where it came from that I have tried to think the feeling was confined to my own small bosom alone; yet that may be not quite the case either. I have a distinct recollection of a fellow pupil at Poppleton's big enough in my eyes to speak with authority, talking of the rival Grammar School with a sort of envy, and using the words "That's a fizzing school."

I had no doubt of it. Once, in Farnham Park, a little group of boys had passed me, looking very daring fellows, and talking with what I thought a most knowing slang; and it was plain they were boarders of the Grammar School, out for a walk with an under-master. Boys to be admired, I felt. To be sure, the Grammar School (in West Street, in the same building now used by the "Girls' Grammar School") had a rather dreadful look. Through the window of "the class-rooms" (demolished long ago), certain desks could be seen from the street (grimy wood, much hacked about with pocket knives I afterwards found out), and I took them to be iron, cold and hard and pitiless. Also the head master, "Old Buffer" (Mr Charles Stroud, whom eventually I learnt to love), seemed to me terrible and stern, with his pursed-up lips and grim overhanging brows and penetrating eyes. But for all that, and having no evidence to go upon, I thoroughly agreed with my stalwart schoolfellow, that the Grammar School was "a fizzing school."

Ambition being thus made to effervesce, I asked my father if I might change; and he, possibly thinking to save trouble, said "Yes; if I would give Mr Poppleton the necessary notice." That, perhaps, ought to have shut me up—for should I not be unwilling to do anything of the sort? In due course, however, being one of a class of little boys sitting in semicircle in front of Mr Poppleton's platform, I held up my hand, and stood up to say "Please, Sir, may I leave?" only to receive an almost unquestioning consent. The awful act had been easy after all. It did not occur to me that Mr Poppleton could hardly raise any difficulties. The thing was done; and I said no more about it to anyone.

But in due time my father knew. In the street he was asked by Mr Poppleton "What are you going to do with George?" "*Do* with him?" My father was puzzled. Was he, Mr Poppleton inquired, proposing to make an artist of him? More than this I don't remember being told about the conversation. That my father was surprised there is no doubt; but it would have been unlike him hastily to suggest any departure from the course I was evidently bent on. Perhaps he himself was a little sick of Mr Poppleton's manner. That there followed any quarrel I never heard; but it is almost certain the schoolmaster felt wounded to the quick.

Probably with reason too. Not that the loss of one pupil would greatly distress him. Certainly he had been always kind to me—had been at pains to make my way comfortable and had treated me with indulgence and, I fancy, personal affection. Also I was not likely to be a discredit to his school.

But the offence went deeper. Even the blow to his vanity was not the worst; though it cannot have been other than painful to such a man to see a rival preferred to him. Worst of all, as I afterwards began to think, my leaving was a threatening symptom of the miserable fate that the years had in store for Mr Poppleton; and the horrible possibility now dawned on him for almost the first time. If he then foresaw his ruin, and held me largely to blame he had more provocation to think so than I had myself, though a time came when, with a conceit worthy of his own, I thought that Mr Poppleton's downfall was the tragic result of my own example to the town, being certainly a bad advertisement. An unquiet conscience insisted that it was my own fault, when years later, Mr Poppleton's school being all gone, and his wife dead, he, lonely and poverty-stricken, had retired to a near village. For many years he would not speak to me, though he took to that again after I had left the Grammar School, and when he was growing old and shabby, and trembling at the lips. One day came word that he had been found dead, starved and dirty and neglected, in the old schoolroom— his only home at last.

I have no recollection of any leave-taking from Mr Poppleton's school. The first thing afterwards that I do recall was my father's taking me into the Grammar School —the schoolroom door opening, and, while talk went on between my father and Mr Stroud, the boys at their desks

looking me over with kindly curiosity. One boy especially
I like to think of now—Ern Beaty. He died later of consumption, but we had time to become great chums first,
and his smile—so frank, so captivating—while he eagerly
patted the seat beside him to get me to sit there and feel
at home, made as delightful a welcome as I ever enjoyed.
It is not my intention to write much about the Grammar
School; but I am glad to recall the mental picture of Ern
Beaty, hitherto a stranger to me, inviting me to sit beside
him and be happy.

Soon I settled down into the new school work, and
thought all was well. If I did not understand the meanings
of *Least Common Multiple* and *Greatest Common Measure*—
things I had never heard of in East Street—at least I soon
learnt the trick of getting the right answers to the problems
proposed. The division of the boys into forms instead of
classes seemed grand. It was also as fine as it was unprecedented to begin and end the day's schooling with
Prayers. I admired the appointment of one boy to be
door-keeper and call out every day the list of late-comers,
with the minutes each had lost. In this connection one
thing puzzled and impressed me very much. "Rule 5,"
"Rule 15," and so on would be called out; and I supposed
that the names that followed belonged to boys who had
broken some regulation not yet known to me as a new boy.
In due time it came out that Rule was the name of a boy.
He lived somewhere outside Farnham and may have been
pardonably late every day. But I was not intimate with
him and didn't feel very much concerned to hear at last

that he had been drowned in Frensham Pond. What could one expect, from a fellow habitually unpunctual? Punctuality was a new idea to me. There was a prize for it. I never won the prize, though I admired the principle. Sometimes, having left home (42 Borough now) while the Town clock was striking, as I ran past the end of the churchyard passage it relieved me that the Church clock still gave me time to reach school by nine; for it was the Church clock we went by; and it was generally slow. That suited me; I liked its tone too. It rang "The Chimes"—"Life let us cherish"—every three hours; and a touch of quiet dignity, as if from an earlier generation, came fitfully but reassuringly from behind the trees across the playground. School was none the worse for occasional snatches of sound from the Church chimes; the town was none the worse for them. The clash and loud jangle of Practice Night—when bell-ringing practice deafened all the near streets—seemed sanctified by that sound.

The playground—sumptuously large it seemed after the little place, not a quarter its size, I had been used to at Poppleton's—had some simple gymnastic apparatus; parallel bars, a horizontal bar, a horizontal ladder. There were always two or three boys clambering about, but I never had pluck enough to be one of them, and moreover dreaded to be laughed at. The games played—eventually I grew too self-conscious to join in them, and walked about shyly; a veritable fogey—the games were what I knew, though their names were strange. What we had called at East Street "Stag," was now "Chevy" or "Prisoner's Base," the "prison" being across the playground in the

234

corner opposite to the base you started from. Having run out and touched an opponent, you said "Go to Buck," and (as there was never any failure to play the game) he meekly went to the "prison." I have wondered since: was this name "Buck" schoolboy English for Bocard?

Another game, "Crown King Caesar," had been known at East Street as "Lion in the Den"; though it was played in the same way. If any "Lion" in the Den would make sure of a catch, he had to hold him, and pat him on the head long enough to say "One, two, three, I crown thee." Otherwise the capture could not be claimed[1].

"Rounders," previously known as "Base-ball," was too competitive for my taste, and drew far too much attention on the individual player. It was more comfortable to be inconspicuous in a "side." "Picking sides" was managed by two leaders alternately choosing. Before them two boys with arms linked offered themselves, asking, "Puddin' or Beef?" whereupon the leader, choosing "Puddin'" or else "Beef," was joined by the boy who answered to that name. Sometimes the choice offered was "Sticks or Stones"; and sometimes some dirty alternative or other, when there would go up a bright-eyed and delighted laugh, and the boys who had the wit to suggest it were the more popular. But for this method of picking sides there was never any other name than "Going in Puddin' or Beef."

[1] By the way, while I was still a very little child this same game made a fine squealing indoor romp called "Sheep, sheep, come home." One player called those words to the other players the other side of the "den." The sheep answered "Fraid." "What are you afraid of?" was the next call: and at the answer, "Wolf," the assurance came "Wolf's gone to Devonshire! Won't be back for seven year." So then the sheep ran across the den and out came the Wolf.

We read the Bible diligently—one verse each all round the class. I also learnt the Church "Catechism," with "Scripture Proofs" of it; so that in due time I could be (and in fact was) confirmed. Very little else was different from Poppleton's; only some of the books were different, as I have already said. The use of maps, and the drawing of maps, made Geography more palatable. In Morell's *Grammar and Analysis* I had been grounded so sensibly by Mr Poppleton that the afternoon lessons in the Grammar School class-room would have been quite agreeable but for one thing. There was a boy I never came in contact with otherwise (one of the Aldershot boys) whose breath often smelt so offensively of the raw onions he was wont to bring with him for his dinner that I disliked the analysis lessons.

A fiercely cultivated disapproval of tale-telling ("sneaking") was one of the best traditions; and may be taken as the end of all I want to say about the Grammar School. It ought perhaps to finish also these memoirs, for in truth my innocent childhood was all but ended. To be sure my childhood was carried over into the Grammar School for all I knew to the contrary then. It was a regret to me that Arthur Nichols went away to a Boarding School when he left the ladies' school he was at, but he was as dear to me as ever. About the same time a little friend of his and mine told me that he too was leaving the same school. "I'm going to Buff's" (Mr Stroud's), he said, "next term." And that seemed to me right and interesting, for I was still a little boy. But for all that the change must have started already.

The change was that I was almost consciously "think-ing" about things. This no doubt began at home. Hearing my brother talk about a certain book to my father, I not only wanted to read that book—to read and talk so much like a grown-up man was what I wanted most of all. So I began to hear of other writers than Kingston and, accordingly, to use my brains.

And in this the Grammar School was helpful, probably more than it quite meant to be. While other boys were benefiting by gymnastics and games fostered by the school, to me, growing too self-conscious and shy to de-light in these aids to development, came and stayed a fascinating delight in quite another development that left infancy behind. I had grown used to being pigeon-breasted, high-shouldered, short of breath, asthmatic. Cricket and football did not appeal to me. The school drill-sergeant, his eyes ablaze, disliked me angrily for standing so badly, and told me I should soon grow pigeon-breasted. But neither he nor anyone took the trouble to find out that that was in fact already the case. I was allowed to believe that "the body" didn't matter. We were extremely pious at the Grammar School. One boy, a Congregationalist, learnt the Church Catechism, because it gave such ad-vantages in the school, where Canon Hoste, the Rector, came every week to give a bible lesson. Orthodox as we could be, we learnt to think lightly of "bodily" matters. It was easy for me, for instance, pigeon-breasted, to sit so crookedly at writing that my misdirected eyes suffered. Nothing mattered but "The Soul," The Intellect.

And here, as already hinted, by happy chance the school

gave me a lift. While I condemned "the body," I acquired deep veneration for "the mind"; wanted to keep it well groomed and agile. And behold, the school in due time furnished me with an example of lovely mind-activity. Algebra had amused me—it seemed so cute. But I was never a mathematician; and when at last I revelled in Euclid the admiration it excited was of an unexpected kind. It was such clean and agile brain work. Though I could not exercise on the horizontal bar, I liked climbing over the *Pons Asinorum*; and if I shed tears over the Thirteenth Proposition, it was because its clearness suggested to me that there must be something more in it, which I was missing altogether. I never got far into the Third Book; but the Second Book charmed me through and through. It seemed so shapely, so perfect; faultless as the "cuttle-bones" on Bognor beach, or as the sparrow's skull in my museum; or as the cast of Greek sculpture at the School of Art. It had its own finished and unimpeachable beauty. Compared to Euclid, a little text-book of "Practical Geometry" seemed too feeble. In trying to draw a heptagon (it was with a view to some examination under the Science and Art Department) I worked my compasses and straight-edge as directed, only to be told by the text-book, "That, or nearly so, is the heptagon required." "*Nearly so!*" I never felt more contemptuous in my life! Euclid never would have tricked me so.

Evidently I was no longer a simple little child.

INDEX

239

INDEX